Bullers
of Milton

Sue Taylor

ACKNOWLEDGEMENTS

It would not have been possible to write this book without contributions from people who worked in Bullers and Allied Insulators and their families. Other individuals and organisations have been generous with their time and resources and I would also like to thank them for their support. In particular I would like to acknowledge the assistance of:

Brian Adams, M. Akhtar, June Alcock, Frank Ashley, Tony Bailey, Graham Bell, Albert Booth, Elizabeth Boothby, Steve Crompton, Bill Davies, Gren Goldstraw, Miranda Goodby, Margaret Hancock, Colin Harris, Diana Harris, Jeremy Harris, Madge Harris, Nigel Harris, Les Higgins, Doris Jeffery, Iris Johnston, Jenifer Jones, Jim Knox, Chris Latimer, Annelise Lawrence, Angela Lee, Adam and John Marshall, Vicky Martin, the late Tony Morley, David Mycock, Bill Picard, James Rushton, James Simcoe and David Swinscoe.

The following organisations have provided access to valuable source material and various members of their staff have gone out of their way to provide assistance whenever required:

Allied Insulators Group Limited, Devon Record Office, Gladstone Working Pottery Museum, The Potteries Museum & Art Gallery, Stoke-on-Trent City Archives, Taylor Tunnicliff Ltd., and the Patents Information Network, Birmingham Central Library.

Photographs of Agnete Hoy and her work courtesy of Annelise Lawrence (Agnete Hoy Collection Archive)

Photograph in memory of Frederick Handley and those of his family who have gone before, supplied by his grandson Anthony.

Finally, I would like to thank Rod Campbell for his encouragement and proof reading and for putting up with all the paper, pots and insulators.

CONTENTS

Bowl decorated by Agnete Hoy and exhibited at the 'Britain Can Make It' exhibition in 1946

Trade advertisement c.1940.

INTRODUCTION

The 19th century saw many great technological developments including the expansion of telegraphy and the production and distribution of electrical power across the world. One of the major Staffordshire companies at the forefront of these developments was Bullers Ltd. of Stoke-on-Trent, electrical porcelain manufacturers.

Most of us have been unconsciously making use of Bullers' technical innovations in our daily lives as we switch on our electrical goods; travel to work by public transport; or make telephone calls. That the name of Bullers is not more famous belies their pivotal role as major electrical porcelain manufacturers of the 19th and 20th centuries and as one of the largest employers and manufacturers in the Staffordshire potteries.

Little has been written about the achievements of this enterprise. Their name is familiar to collectors of railway and telegraph memorabilia who buy and exchange Bullers' insulators across the globe. An exhibition of the work of their art pottery studio (1932-1952) was held at the Gladstone Pottery Museum in Stoke-on-Trent in 1977 and a catalogue was published to accompany this. (Now out of print) A demand is now growing for these decorative wares amongst those collecting the antiques of the future.

This book charts the establishment of the company by the Buller family and its later work under the management of the Harris family. It examines the range of products manufactured from the 19th century through to the renaming of the enterprise as Allied Insulators in 1959 and the eventual closure of the Milton factory in 2001.

Sue Taylor
Calton
September 2002

Courtesy of Taylor Tunnicliff Ltd

View of Milton Works c.1925-30 looking towards Baddeley Green

RULES & REGULATIONS

TO BE OBSERVED

IN THIS MANUFACTORY.

1. The Working Hours for the Week as under :—

	A. M.	P. M.
Monday, Tuesday & Wednesday,	6 30 to	6 0
Thursday and Friday - -	6 0 to	6 0
Saturday - - - -	6 0 to	1 30

	S.	D.
2. Any person passing in or out of the Works at any other than the appointed entrance, in the Working Hours, shall be fined - - - - -	0	6
3. For going out of the Works at any other than the appointed times, without permission from the Manager - -	0	3
4. For drinking *Spirits or Fermented Liquors,* or being intoxicated, or for bringing in *Malt* Liquors or *Spirits* -	1	0
5. For introducing a stranger into the Works without permission - - -	1	0
6. For bringing a Dog into the Works	0	3
7. For taking *Chips* out of the Works without leave - - - - -	0	3
8. For taking Tools out of the Works, the value of them, and - - -	0	6
9. For injuring a Machine or Tool through wantonness, or neglect, the expense of repairing it - - - -		

	S.	D.
10. For striking any person in the Works - - - - - -	0	6
11. For swearing or making use of other bad language - - - -	0	6
12. For ordering any *Tool* or *Materials* without being duly authorized - -	0	6
13. The enlarging any holes in the Gas-burners - - - - -	0	3
14. For throwing Clay - - -	0	3
15. For reading any book or newspaper in the working hours, or unnecessarily wasting time in conversation or otherwise - - - - -	0	3
16. For leaving a window open at night - - - - - -	0	3
17. For tearing or otherwise defacing these Regulations - - - -	0	3
18. Windows found broken will be charged to the parties working in the *same Workshop,* unless the person who did the damage be ascertained.		
19. Boys' and Girls' Fines to be only one-half, excepting in the Rule which applies to the Breaking of Windows, in which case the full Fine will be levied.		

☞ The above Regulations are intended solely for the purpose of maintaining better order in these Works, preventing wasteful and unnecessary expense, and for promoting the good conduct and respectability of the Workpeople. In all cases will the Fines be strictly enforced, and the proceeds paid into the Sick Club.

W. W. BULLER & CO.

ALLBUT AND DANIEL, PRINTERS, HANLEY.

1868.

Chapter 1

THE FORMATION OF THE COMPANY

THE BULLERS

The Buller family lived and worked in the West Country (Devon and Cornwall) for over three centuries. They were wealthy landowners, being descended from Sir Richard Buller who was Member of Parliament for, and Sheriff of, Cornwall in 1637. The succeeding generations of the Buller men remained active in Parliament as members of the Liberal (Whig) Party and were also well represented as officers in the armed forces. Towards the end of the 18th century there were thirteen Bullers serving as Members of Parliament at one time. The family had a reputation as responsible and supportive landlords and were known for their involvement in charitable and social causes.

The first Buller linked to the manufacture of pottery was Captain Thomas Wentworth Buller, described in 1850 as *"Lord of the manors of Whimple, Strete Raleigh and Cobdon"*[1]. Strete Raleigh had 128 inhabitants and the Bullers (presumably Thomas's father William) had bought this property in 1794.[2] Thomas Wentworth was a Captain in the navy, serving on board H.M.S. Bedford during the siege of New Orleans in 1815.[3] In 1836 he served as one of three Commissioners on the Tithe Commission which had been established following the Tithe Commutation Act.[4] An 1822 source lists him as from Northamptonshire but owning Cobden between 1822 and 1850.[5] In his 1849 patent his address is listed as Sussex Gardens, London[6] and from another source we know that this was also a home address, near Hyde Park.[7] It would therefore appear that he owned at least three residences - in Devon, in Northamptonshire and in London.

His involvement in the pottery industry can be traced back to 1843 when he and his brother-in-law John Divett took out a lease on the Folly Pottery in Devon, under the partnership name Buller, Divett and Company, renaming it The Bovey Tracey Pottery Company.[8] A later company letterhead also states that the company was established in Devonshire in 1843.[9] They made earthenwares which were described by a writer of the times as of a quality equal to the ordinary, inexpensive wares produced in Staffordshire.[10] These included white, printed and coloured wares for the home markets in the west of England but also for export to Mediterranean ports including Malta.

Within this pottery existed a separate enterprise referred to in the literature as the 'Spur Works', solely owned by Thomas Wentworth Buller.[10A] They made ceramic kiln furniture such as spurs and stilts as shown in an 1849 patent taken out by Thomas Wentworth Buller for the production of moulded cockspurs as an improvement to the existing process for hand-finished cockspurs. The contents of this patent, entitled *Improvements in the Manufacture of Earthenware,* suggest that the business also included the production of goods such as jelly cans, toy tea cups and other decorative earthenware.

The original works in Devon were enlarged until they were firing on average five glost ovens per week which suggests a high rate of production. The fuel used was originally lignite, obtained locally, but as the works grew the supply of lignite was not sufficient for their needs and coal from Somerset was brought in by railway to replace it.[12]

T.W. Buller was chosen to exhibit at the 1851 Great Exhibition in the Crystal Palace, London. He exhibited three items in Class 1, Mining and Mineral Products, listed as:

- Specimens of lignite or Bovey coal.
- Specimens of earthenware fired with this coal.
- Patent stilts and cockspurs used in the manufacture of earthenware.

According to the catalogue it was the only instance in which lignite (bituminized wood) had been successfully applied to the firing of earthenware in England.[12A]

Thomas Wentworth Buller paid at least one visit to Staffordshire prior to the company moving north. Around the end of 1848 or early in 1849 he was taken on a tour of pottery establishments by a paper manufacturer from Hanley, a Mr. Fourdrinier, to see the latest processes being used. (Fourdrinier manufactured the tissue paper used in the pottery industry for transferring inked designs from engraved colour plates to earthenware. The Bovey Tracey Pottery may have been one of his customers). During the patent infringement proceedings of 1850 (see chapter 2) a witness (Mr Edward Whalley of Hanley) stated that he had purchased cockspurs and pins from an agent of Bullers for a penny a gross.[13] This confirms that Bullers were actively involved in selling to the Staffordshire potters in advance of their expansion north.

Thomas Wentworth Buller died in 1852 leaving his son Wentworth William as the heir to Strete Raleigh and his business interests, which included the Bovey Tracey Pottery Co.[13A] In 1860 Wentworth William Buller took into partnership Jabez Hearn Mugford, who had been the manager of the Spur Works.[14] The partnership was specifically for *"the manufacture of patent cockspurs, stilts and pins used in the manufacture of earthenware"*[15]. The company extended their business north to Staffordshire in 1860[16] where they eventually became involved in electrical porcelain production. The decision to expand to Staffordshire, away from an area of rich clay deposits, may have been based on ease of access to better quality coal supplies in Staffordshire and also to be nearer to the majority of the consumers of their products. They acquired a twenty year lease on premises at Joiners Square, Hanley.[16A]

On the 28th November 1862, Buller and Mugford are listed as registering a patent for spur-supporting rings[17], and in an 1864 directory of Staffordshire businesses, the company is listed as *"Buller, Mugford & Co. Patent cockspur, stilt & c., manufacturers, Joiner's Square"*.[18]

Between 1864 and 1866 Mugford sold his half share in the business to John Divett and the company became W.W. Buller & Co. Ernest Wentworth Buller (Lieutenant of the Royal Regiment of Artillery) and William Templer Hughes (Colonel in H.M. Indian Army, later Brigadier General) bought Divett's share, equally divided, for the sum of £3496. 1s 5d. each. Hughes was married to Catharine, Wentworth William's sister. Family papers note that Ernest Wentworth had been advanced a total of £3500 from his father's will and he used this money to buy into his cousin's business following an unfortunate accident whilst serving abroad. On 31st October 1868 Wentworth William Buller retired from the business leaving as sole partners Ernest Buller and William Hughes and the company then became Buller & Co.[19]

Ernest Wentworth Buller was a nephew of Thomas Wentworth and therefore cousin to Wentworth William. As noted above he was in the Royal Regiment of Artillery and in an account of the town of Hanley it states that he was a civil engineer who had returned from an appointment under the Indian Government after an accident.[20] A biography of General Sir

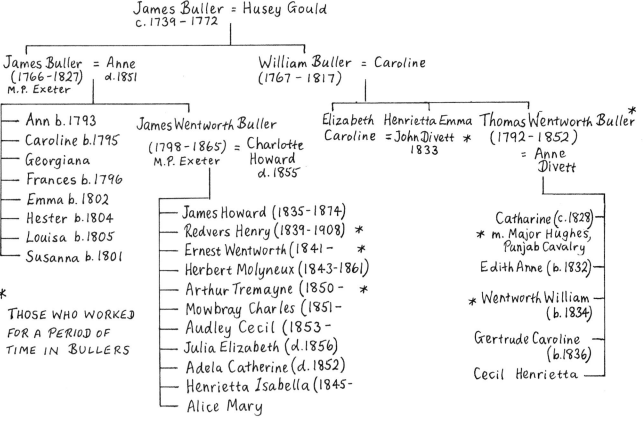

Extract from family tree of Buller of Downes

Redvers Buller states that this accident involved Ernest being chewed 27 times by a lion and being lucky to survive![21] This same source notes him as the founder of a china works in Staffordshire, but this is clearly incorrect.

By 1870 the company is listed in the Hanley section of J.G. Harrod & Co.'s directory as Buller & Co. and their activities described thus:

"BULLER & CO., manufacturers of earthenware, thimble cockspurs, stilts, pins, cup rings, claws and every sort of placing goods for potters' use, china, mortice, rim, and latch furniture, finger plates, shutter, drawer, and centre knobs, vitrified castor bowls, and every description of china for the brassfounders, cabinet, and metallic bedstead trades, &c., insulators, battery plates, cells and all kinds of electric telegraph ware, mortars, pestles &c., depot, 23 Congreve Street, Birmingham".[22]

Kelly's Directory for 1876 lists the company in the Birmingham Commercial Section:

"Buller & Co. - telegraph patentees & contractors to Government Post office, railway & telegraph companies; manufacturers of insulators, mortars & pestles, all kinds of rim, mortice & latch furniture, finger plates; shutter, drawer, commode, cupboard & centre door knobs & every description of china used by tin plate workers, bedstead makers, plumbers & brass founders, every pattern of placing goods for potters' use. 211 Sherlock Street; Hanley, Staffordshire Potteries; & 132 Upper Thames St. London."[23]

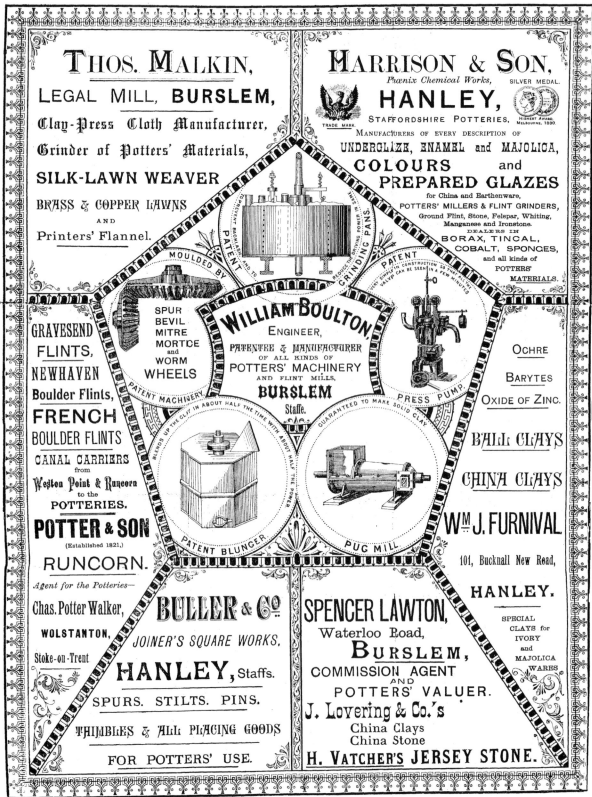

Advertisement from Furnival's *Explanation of the Staffordshire Potteries Slop Flint and Stone Calculator*, 1884.

Company Advertisement c.1870.   Courtesy of Taylor Tunnicliff Ltd

In an 1884 directory the company is again listed as Buller & Co. and this time described as *"Door Furniture makers - China"*.[24]

An article written in 1931 reports that in 1883 Ernest Wentworth Buller asked engineer John Thomas Harris to become his partner.[25] However, Buller family papers suggest that this association was actually formed in 1873 with Harris receiving a salary of £300 per annum.[26] Descendants of John Harris believed that Buller had suggested the partnership on the basis that Harris had the brains and he, Buller, had the finance. Later reports in the scientific press suggest that Harris's contribution was to be the establishment of an engineering department which could provide the metal components for the insulator manufacturing part of the business which was by then a developing area.

The name of the company changed again in 1885 when Buller and Harris entered into partnership with Howard Cochrane Jobson who owned a business at the Phoenix Works in Dudley known as Jobson Bros.[27] This company employed 27 men and 48 boys.[28] The new company was legally constituted on 8th June 1885 and was called Buller, Jobson & Co. Ltd. and they continued to manufacture not only insulators but also the metal fittings necessary to fix or support the ceramic insulators and the metal poles and brackets to carry them.

The Agreement between the three partners in this new company lists their individual skills as follows:

"Howard Cochrane Jobson of Dudley in the County of Worcester Engineer, Telegraphic Engineer Ironfounder and Contractor and Ernest Wentworth Buller of Birmingham in the County of Warwick and John Thomas Harris of Hanley in the County of Stafford Potters, Metal Workers and Contractors."

The Agreement does suggest that the partners will carry on their respective businesses in their current locations and that the new company is simply an official and convenient merging of existing resources and businesses. The assets of Jobson Brothers were £8881.11s.4d whilst Buller & Co. had assets of £13813.1s.6d.

In the Memorandum of Association dated 8th June 1885, the list of initial subscribers to the formation of the company, with one share apiece, reads as follows:

Howard Cochrane Jobson. 196 Wolverhampton Street, Dudley, Worcestershire. Engineer.
Edward Percy Jobson. 199 Wolverhapmton Street, Dudley, Worcestershire. Solicitor.
Ernest Wentworth Buller. 49 Charlotte Road, Edgbaston, Birmingham. Manufacturer.
William Steward Forster. 20 Lincoln's Inn Fields, London. Solicitor.
Redvers Henry Buller. Downes, Devon. Major General.
Arthur Tremayne Buller. Greystoke, Cumberland. Gentleman.
William Greenhill. 65 Colmore Road, Birmingham. Bank Manager.
John T. Harris. Eastwood House, Hanley, Staffordshire.

Ernest Buller was the Chairman, Howard Jobson the Deputy Chairman (to be Buller's successor) and John Harris was a Director. Redvers Henry Buller and Arthur Tremayne Buller were brothers of Ernest and most probably sleeping partners in the business, as Redvers was pursuing a successful military career and Arthur lived in Cumbria. Edward Jobson was Howard's brother.

An 1889 gazetteer and directory for Hanley lists the company as *"spur, stilt, door furniture, mortar and pestle and telegraph insulater [sic] manufacturers, Joiner's square"*[29], confirming that the

8859

8 JUN 1885

An Agreement made this twentieth day of May One thousand eight hundred and eighty five Between Howard Cochrane Jobson of Dudley in the County of Worcester Engineer, Telegraphic Engineer Ironfounder and Contractor and Ernest Wentworth Buller of Birmingham in the County of Warwick and John Thomas Harris of Hanley in the County of Stafford Potters Metal Workers and Contractors and Copartners (all of whom are hereinafter collectively referred to as "the Vendors") of the one part and Edward Percy Jobson of Dudley aforesaid Solicitor as a Trustee on behalf of a Company intended to be incorporated under the Companies Acts 1862 to 1883 as a Company Limited by Shares with the name of "Buller Jobson & Co Limited" (hereinafter referred to as "the Company") of the other part Whereby it is recorded and agreed as follows vide licet

1. Howard Cochrane Jobson carries on business as an Engineer, Telegraphic Engineer, Ironfounder and Contractor at Dudley aforesaid under the style of "Jobson Brothers"

2. Ernest Wentworth Buller and John Thomas Harris carry on business as Potters, Metal

Field Roscoe ?
36 Lincoln Inn Fields

Agreement dated 20th May 1885 between Ernest Buller, John Harris and Howard Jobson.

The Schedule

Particulars of Allotment in Bullers Limited ... above referred to ... _in respect of shares in Buller, Jobson & Co Limited_

Names of shareholders	Addresses and Descriptions	Amount paid or credited as paid on Shares in Bullers Limited £	Amount paid or credited as paid on Shares in Buller Jobson & Co Limited £	No. Preferred Shares in each Co. allotted in Bullers Limited	No. Preferred Shares in each Co. allotted in Buller Jobson & Co Limited	No. Ordinary Shares in each Co. allotted in Buller Jobson & Co Limited	Amount to be paid in Cash	Distinctive numbers of preferred shares	Distinctive numbers of ordinary shares
Ernest Wentworth Buller	114 Charlotte Road, Edgbaston, Birmingham, Engineer	24,500	5,000	13444	13444	13444	£1.12.3	1 to 13444	1 to 13444
Howard Graham Jobson	Summer Hill, Kidderminster, Engineer	44,500	9,000	2633	2633	2633	£9.7.9	13445 to 14533	13445 to 14533
John Thomas Harris	The Hayes, Stone, Staffordshire, Engineer	11,000	3,000	1145	1145	1145	£7.15.3	14533 to 5677	14533 to 5677
Edward John Chambers	Dudley, Worcestershire, Engineer	500		25	25	25		5677 to 5702	5677 to 5702
Arthur Kent Sharp	37 St James Place, London, B.A. Cambridge	500		25	25	25		5703 to 5727	5703 to 5727
Edward Percy Jobson	Dudley, Worcestershire, Solicitor	24		1	1	1		5728	5728
William Howard Foster	24 Lincolns Inn Fields, London, Solicitor	24		1	1	1		5729	5729
Arthur Wentworth Buller	Gropstoke Church, Land Agent	24		1	1	1		5730	5730
William Greenhill	Dudley, Worcestershire, Bank Manager	24		1	1	1		5731	5731

Witness to the signatures of Arthur Wentworth Buller [and] Howard Graham Buller — [signatures]

Witness to the signatures of Ernest Wentworth Buller, Howard Graham Jobson, Walter Winston Fisher, John Chambers, John Thomas Harris — [signatures]

Witness to the signatures of William Greenhill and Edward Percy Jobson — [signatures]

The Common Seal of Buller, Jobson & Co Limited was hereunto affixed in the presence of — [signatures]

The Common Seal of Bullers Limited was hereunto affixed in the presence of ... _Directors_

Allotment of shares in Bullers Ltd following voluntary liquidation of Buller, Jobson & Co Ltd 1890.

metal foundry work was not located in Hanley. This arrangement of operating two factories - one in the Black Country and one in the Potteries - continued well into the 20th century.

In 1890 the company changed its name to Bullers Ltd. and was formally incorporated on 6th October as a private company.[30] Buller, Jobson & Co. was placed into voluntary liquidation in order that the company might be reconstructed and a new issue of 20,000 shares be offered at £10 each. The shareholders in the old company who were entitled to receive new shares are listed as:

Ernest W. Buller - original investment £34,920 - 1844 ordinary & 1844 preference shares
Howard C. Jobson - original investment £50,500 - 2688 ordinary & 2688 preference shares
John T. Harris - original investment £21,600 - 1145 ordinary & 1145 preference shares
Edward J. Chambers - original investment £500 - 25 ordinary & 25 preference shares
Arthur K. Tharp - original investment £500 - 25 ordinary & 25 preference shares
William Greenhill - original investment £20 - 1 ordinary share & 1 preference share
Edward P. Jobson - original investment £20 - 1 ordinary share & 1 preference share
William S. Forster - original investment £20 - 1 ordinary share & 1 preference share
Arthur T. Buller - original investment £20 - 1 ordinary share & 1 preference share

They appear to have bought out a previous shareholder entitled Howard Proctor Rylands. A further reconstruction took place in 1896 but the company name remained the same. In 1895 the Sherlock Street offices in Birmingham closed and all business was transferred from there and the Phoenix Works in Dudley to the New Works at Tipton.[31] The new works was located in Factory Road close to the railway and canal.

THE HARRIS FAMILY

Although the company continued to trade under the name of Bullers, the descendants of John Thomas Harris were the shareholders and managers who most influenced the development of the company and its products in Stoke-on-Trent during the 20th century. Four generations of the Harris family worked within the company during this period thus following a Staffordshire pottery industry tradition of family-run businesses.

In 1885 John Harris was living in Eastwood House, Hanley.[32] This property belonged to the company and was located a short distance uphill from the factory. The 1901 census shows his first four children as being born in Hanley. As the company prospered and his wealth and status increased, he moved out of the Potteries to the town of Stone prior to 1890, first to The Hayes and later to The Radfords. A measure of his financial success is the fact that in 1903 he purchased Yarlet Hall as a wedding present for his daughter Ellen and her future husband John Fernie to run as a school for boys. The family connection with this establishment was maintained as succeeding generations of Harris children also attended the school.[33]

John T. Harris was succeeded in the business by his four sons - John Waugh, Gilbert, Neill and Ralph Guy. John Waugh Harris is reported as Works Manager at Hanley in 1905[34], later succeeding his father as Managing Director and Chairman. Gilbert Harris became one of the company management team at Hanley, whilst Neill ran the Tipton works. Of particular importance to the later artistic work of the company was John T. Harris's youngest son Guy who, following an accident which ended his chosen career in agriculture, came to the works as a chemist and later became Technical Director.

John Waugh Harris died in 1920 aged only 46. He had been Chairman of the Spur and Stilt Association and his social and political interests included being District Secretary of the NSPCC, Justice of the Peace for the County of Stafford, and a Deacon of Stone Congregational Church. He had four sons and one daughter.[35]

The workforce demonstrated their respect for John Waugh Harris both during his life and after his death. In 1894, to mark the occasion of his 21st birthday, they presented him with an illuminated manuscript, a gold watch and a set of hunting harness. (The text of this manuscript can be found in Appendix 1).

His life was also commemorated by the company's donation of a tiled hallway for the entrance hall of the Royal Infirmary, Hartshill, Stoke-on-Trent, the central plaque of which is shown on page 17.

E Boothby & D Harris

John Thomas Harris.

Just prior to his death, he purchased the house The Hayes for £13,000, hoping to re-establish this as the Harris home again. It had been sold outside the family by John Thomas and it had been John Waugh's long held ambition to buy it back. Sadly, he didn't live long enough to enjoy it.

Gilbert Harris suceeded John Waugh as Chairman and continued in this role until his sixties, when he was replaced by John Elvine Harris, John Waugh's son. John Elvine was joined in the company by his brother Donald ('Sam') who had trained as an automotive engineer with Leyland in South Africa but returned to Bullers after the Second World War. His role was managing the department which made smaller low tension insulating components. Their brother Reginald Waugh also worked briefly at Bullers but chose instead to pursue an artistic career. He attended Burslem School of Art and is believed to have designed some tableware for a Longton factory and to have made furniture for the retail market in London. He also rode in the Grand National.

Guy Harris was actively involved in the local ceramic industry societies and held the position of President of the British Ceramic Society in 1947-48, having been a member of the Society for over 40 years. He also served on the Council of the British Ceramic Research Association and was Chairman of its Electrical Porcelain Panel, publishing technical papers on vitrification, saggars and kiln furniture.[36]

Those who worked in the factory remember the Harris family with both respect and affection, describing them as "gentlemen" who cared about their enterprise and knew all their employees by name. They were known to the workforce as "Mr Gilbert", "Mr Guy" etc, a convention which is still found in some companies in the Potteries to this day. In those early days of the 20th century the social and employment hierarchy was clear and accepted by all and there appears to have been little dissatisfaction amongst the workforce. Gilbert Harris is remembered as walking through all parts of the factory every day, keeping abreast of what was happening and speaking to the staff. When he lost two sons in the Second World War (Richard Waugh Harris in 1940 and David Carrington Harris in 1943), as a mark of respect the staff contributed to the purchase of a cot in the North Staffordshire Royal Infirmary. The company also paid for the tiles in the entrance hall of the Royal Infirmary at Hartshill and a plaque is there to mark this donation.[37]

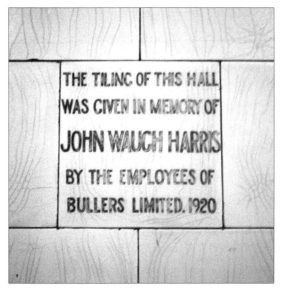

Tiling in the main entrance hall of North Staffordshire Royal Infirmary, manufactured by Corn Bros.

The senior managers of the company did not live in Milton itself or near the factory. Following the example of John T. Harris they chose to live in the countryside around the Leek area, in villages such as Bradnop, Stanley and Endon. They, of course, had the benefit of company cars, and, in the 1930s and 1940s, for the most senior partners, a company chauffeur called Robert Pierpont was on call. Some junior employees remember being taken home in these cars if they had missed their bus because of being asked to work late. For the rest of the workforce travel by bus from Hanley, on bicycle or on foot was the norm. Six or seven buses ran between Milton and Hanley to convey the large number of workers who had transferred from Joiner's Square, whilst other buses served Baddeley Green and surrounding areas.

E Boothby & D Harris

E Boothby & D Harris

John Thomas Harris at The Hayes, Stone.

Right: John Waugh Harris.

Below: John Thomas Harris outside his home again.

E Boothby & D Harris

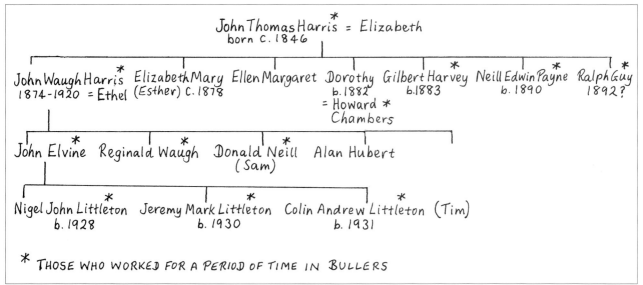

John Thomas Harris * = Elizabeth
born c. 1846

John Waugh Harris * Elizabeth Mary Ellen Margaret Dorothy Gilbert Harvey * Neill Edwin Payne * Ralph Guy *
1874-1920 = Ethel (Esther) c. 1878 b.1882 b.1883 b.1890 1892?
= Howard *
Chambers

John Elvine * Reginald Waugh * Donald Neill * Alan Hubert
(Sam)

Nigel John Littleton * Jeremy Mark Littleton * Colin Andrew Littleton * (Tim)
b. 1928 b. 1930 b. 1931

* THOSE WHO WORKED FOR A PERIOD OF TIME IN BULLERS

Extract from Harris family tree.

After the war, John Elvine's sons Nigel, Colin (Tim) and Jeremy joined him at Bullers, Nigel in 1950, Colin in 1953 and Jeremy in 1954. After leaving the forces, Nigel enrolled on the Pottery Managers' Course at the Stoke-on-Trent Technical College and, to complement this, was sent to work in different areas of the Milton factory to learn how the company products were made. From this shop floor introduction to the company he then moved into management before leaving in 1963 to become a partner in Alton Towers.

Colin Harris spent two years at Oxford University before choosing to return to the family business and joined the Tipton factory in 1953 where his uncle, Neill Harris, was Managing Director. During his time there in the 1950s as Assistant Works Manager many improvements were carried out to what was a collection of very run down buildings with old fashioned equipment. New metalworking machinery was installed and a fleet of fork lift trucks were purchased. An ex-army lorry travelled to Milton once a week carrying fittings.

Guy Harris, in his beloved Staffordshire Moorlands c. 1960.

E Boothby & D Harris

John Elvine's youngest son, Jeremy, trained as an accountant. He worked at Tipton between 1959 and 1963 as Works' Accountant before moving to Twyfords.

John Elvine Harris and his uncle
Gilbert Harris c. 1947.

C.A.L. Harris

John Elvine Harris died in 1965 and his shares in the company were left to his sons. Prior to this, changes had been made to the structure of the company and the composition of the management team. Nigel and Jeremy Harris had already left Bullers in 1963, and Colin followed soon after. All three brothers relinquished their share and this effectively ended the family involvement in the running of the company.

OTHER KEY PERSONNEL

In the 1881 census Isaac Pennell is listed as Pottery Manager living at 14 Eastwood Place, beside the Joiner's Square Works. He originated from Devon and so may have been acquainted with the Bullers there. In 1891 his name appeared with that of John Harris on a patent for kiln furniture[38]. In the 1901 census he is still resident in Hanley but now at Eastwood House previously occupied by John Harris. His son Frank, listed in the census as a newspaper clerk, later followed his father into the business and registered a patent in 1925 concerned with the apparatus for pugging (or extruding) clay.[39] By the 1930s one of the Pennells was managing both the Milton and Hanley factories and the family by now lived at Endon in a large property with tennis courts.

At the Tipton site in 1891 the Managing Director (and one of the shareholders) was Edward J. Chambers[40] whilst his son, Howard Chambers, was Works Manager by 1905.[41] The 1901 Census lists Edward J. Chambers' profession as 'Civil and Mechanical Engineer and Managing Director of Engineering Works'. Howard is listed as 'Mechanical Engineer and Manager Telegraph Engineering Works'. Both men registered designs for metal telegraph poles.[42] John Thomas Harris's daughter Dorothy married Howard Chambers[43], thus bringing the two business partners closer together. The Tipton situation in those early days almost exactly mirrored the father-son working hierarchy at Milton. Howard's brother Frederick is also believed to have been in a managerial position. The Assistant Manager at Tipton was W.E. Bamfield and the Company Secretary T.H. Simmonds. When Neill Harris retired as Managing Director of Tipton, he was succeeded by Mr Tolley, the Works' Inspector. Later the Managing Director at Tipton was Mr. W. Bourne, whose son George also worked there. When he retired he was replaced by a Mr. Hearsum.

The management at Tipton also had the privilege of access to a company car. Mr Bourne had a 1928 Austin 20 and then changed it for a Rolls Royce. The company driver was Reg Vincent who had started work at Tipton as a horse and cart driver. When the company purchased its first motor vehicle, a Daimler, he had to be sent to the Daimler factory to learn how to drive.

Bullers Limited had a head office in London where the overall Chairman of the company, Hubert Charles Rayner Dagnall, was based. It is not clear how or when he assumed this position. He had been in the company since before 1932 as his name appears on patents of that date. Although his trade on the 1901 census is listed as electrical engineer, his role was thought to be managerial rather than technical and the patents may simply have been registered in his name on behalf of the company. His son John was also a salesman in the London office. John Elvine Harris was required to travel to London for meetings with Mr Dagnall and other board members. It is thought that Mr Dagnall did not come to Staffordshire very often - apparently he did not even attend the annual company dinners.

In the 1950s at Milton the Board was chaired by Gilbert Harris and, as well as other family members already mentioned, it now also included the qualified engineers, Bill Robinson and George Perrins, who had been with the company since the 1930s and had demonstrated their technical expertise in the design of insulators, registering several patents.

THE WORKFORCE

Bullers were one of the two main employers in the locality of Milton, the other being British Aluminium. At Bullers, as with other employers of the period, the pattern was for members of a family to follow their parents or other family elders into the firm, being recommended or spoken for to the management as potential employees. Many families therefore had several members employed in the company, with sons and daughters following their parents into employment there. A good example of this can be found in the Davies family where four brothers worked - one as the plumber, two as joiners, and one in the grinding shop. The plumber's assistant was his son who later succeeded his father as the senior plumber. Employees tended to remain with the company until retirement and so promotion frequently only occurred when the senior tradesman retired and the younger ex-apprentice moved up. A job at Bullers was generally considered to be "a job for life".

THE WORKS

The original site chosen by the company for their works was at Joiner's Square in Hanley, Stoke-on-Trent, adjacent to what is now known as the Caldon Canal and with easy access to a main road. Thomas Hargreaves' map of 1832[44] shows the area around Joiner's Square as open land with two wharves and two collieries nearby. It also clearly shows Eastwood House which is given as the address for John Harris in 1885.[45] An unpublished written source reports three bottle ovens in existence in 1865, with this increasing to twelve by 1910. The 1924 Ordnance Survey map shows this as an area of high industrialisation, with three flint and stone mills conveniently located on the canal nearby. The factory was known within the company as Joiner's Square Works, but also referred to in the historical ceramic literature as Eastwood Vale.[46] One bottle oven still remains standing on the site, preserved as part of a new housing development by Stoke on Trent Housing Society and entitled the 'Bottlekiln'. The author was able to confirm this as part of the original factory by the retrieval of dated and stamped insulators from the building site in 1999.

The company maintained a London office at 6 Laurence Pountney Hill, Cannon Street, London with agencies in Glasgow, Australia, South Africa, Mexico, India and Spain. An early

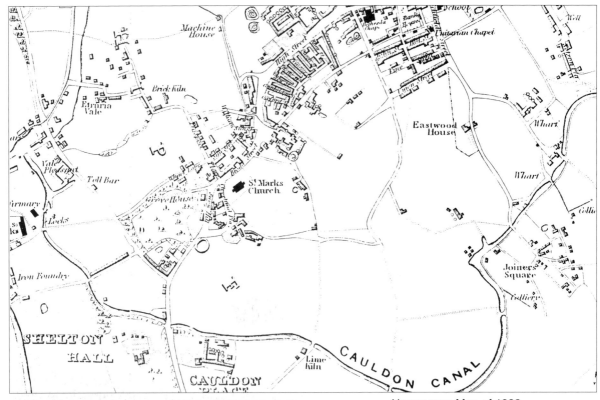

Hargreaves Map of 1832.

catalogue states that they were contractors to H.M. Post Office; Admiralty; War Office; India Office; Colonial and Foreign Governments; Railway, Telegraph and Telephone Companies.[47]

By the turn of the century however, Bullers' works at Joiner's Square, like many other factories in the Potteries, occupied what had become a very overcrowded site on the canal side. There was little or no room for the much needed expansion of production facilities on this site and the company had to look outside of the city for a suitable new location. The new site chosen was at Milton, a rural location a few miles north of the city centre and so, just prior to the First World War, plans were made to move to this new, purpose built factory. The move was, in fact, postponed until after the

Bottle oven at Bullers' Hanley Works during renovation and incorporation into residential premises 2001.

war. The new factory opened in 1920 and, according to the Financial Times in 1930:

"The Milton works provide an outstanding example of emplacement and arrangement of modern ceramic plant, the whole 'layout' having been expressly conceived with a view to ensuring direct sequence of each stage of production."[48]

This form of factory design would nowadays be the norm but, when compared to the haphazard arrangement of its Stoke-on-Trent contemporaries, the new works would have given Bullers a distinct competitive advantage. To ensure good communication links the factory was built adjacent to the North Staffordshire Railway and the Trent and Mersey Canal (Caldon Branch) and Leek New Road. The raw ingredients were originally brought to the works at Milton by rail and canal, the factory having its own railway siding and wharf. It is uncertain when use of the canal ceased, but it seems likely to have been in the 1940s. The company plumber, who started work in 1939, remembered it being in use, the clay coming in by canal barge and being shovelled onto a wooden barrow and wheeled off to the blungers.

On the 1925 Ordnance Survey map (see p. 28) the new factory is shown with the railway spur, wharf and three bottle ovens depicted in diagrammatic form, corroborating the unpublished evidence above. Although surrounded by apparently agricultural land, maps show the start of some new residential development to the south of the area.

The equivalent map of 1937 (see p. 29) shows considerable extensions to the works with an additional three ovens having been built separate from the main works and new buildings adjacent to the canal. Housing developments can be seen south of Leek New Road and to the north east at Milton. Much of this housing was of reasonable quality, with garden areas. A new sewage works to the east of the factory is evidence of an increasing population. The Financial Times of 1930 reported that there were 2000 employees working for Bullers at that time [49] and many of these would have

The fettling shop at Hanley Works c. 1908.

been resident in the Milton and Baddeley Green area.

The 1961 (see p. 42) and 1967 Ordnance Survey maps show more expansion utilising most of the available land - indeed the 1961 map suggests that the northern boundary may have been extended. Two contractors who worked on the site in 1969 stated: *"The first impression of the Bullers factory is size - a labyrinth of buildings."*[50]

The New Works at Tipton were opened in 1895 and the company continued to operate from that original site. All metal components were manufactured there. Some were transported to Stoke-on-Trent for assembly and fitting to insulators. These arrived once a week on an ex-army lorry.

The Tipton works were never modernised in the same way as the Stoke-on-Trent factories. Working conditions there were always somewhat unpleasant and more dangerous, as can be seen from early photographs. Some improvements were made in the 1950s and new equipment purchased, but areas of the works were still old. The galvanising shop was particularly bad. It suffered from a leaking roof and fumes from the acid tanks. Their office was a shed on three wheels which had been the architect's office when the factory was first built.

A range of items found on the Joiners Square site during redevelopment work in 2001-02, including kiln furniture, ink well cover, drawer knob, light switch, spark plug component.

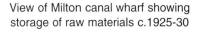

BULLERS
LIMITED,
6 LAURENCE POUNTNEY HILL, CANNON STREET,
LONDON, E.C.

Telegraphic Address:
"BULLERS, LONDON."

REGISTERED
TRADE MARK.

Telephone Nos.:
4907/8 LONDON WALL.

Iron Works:
Tipton, Staffordshire.

Porcelain Works:
Hanley, Staffordshire.

Contractors to: H.M. POST OFFICE, ADMIRALTY, WAR OFFICE, INDIA OFFICE, COLONIAL AND FOREIGN GOVERNMENTS, RAILWAY, TELEGRAPH AND TELEPHONE COMPANIES.

AGENCIES:

GLASGOW - - - James Dick, 19 Waterloo Street.

AUSTRALIA - - A. J. Chamberlin & Co., 350 Little Collins St., Melbourne.

SOUTH AFRICA - Jenkins & Co., Holts Buildings, 352, Smith Street, Durban.
  „ P.Y.E. Chambers, 51 Long Street, Cape Town.
  „ 175 Main Street, P.O. Box 654, Johannesburg.

MEXICO - - - W. Young & Co., Calle de Gante, No. 11 Mexico City.

INDIA - - - - Bullers Ltd., 10 Upper Clive Street, Calcutta.

SPAIN - - - - The Peninsular Engineering Co., Ltd., 241 Calle de Valencia, 241 (esquina Rambla de Cataluna), Barcelona.

ENTERED AT STATIONERS' HALL.   COPYRIGHT REGISTERED.

Front page of an early undated Bullers' sales catalogue.

View of Milton canal wharf showing storage of raw materials c.1925-30

Courtesy of Taylor Tunnicliff Ltd

TIPTON TRANSPORT

Outside the furniture shop, Tipton works. Twin cylinder 6HP Daimler bought June 1901, before number plates. Bunsen burner ignition, pressure kept up by valve in exhaust. Surface wick carburettor. Automatic inlet valves. 4 speeds forward, 4 reverse. Chain drive, solid tyres. The tyres kept coming off. Speed 20 mph. To start, a cycle pump was used to fill the cups under the burners (like present day blow lamps). Canvas top body painted chocolate with yellow letters. Oil lighting. 12 mpg petrol (11d per gallon). First commercial vehicle in the Midlands. It was used for about 3 years, carrying 2 tons. The driver spent a month at Coventry learning to drive, but was 'never much good'. The canvas top was taken off each morning and the van used for internal transport. Repairs £362 in 3 years, including £71 for accident (1902) and £46 for overhaul May 1904, after which it was sold. Driver's wages £87 p.a. Insurance 25/- p.a. License (car and man) 25/. Cost per cwt delivered over 3 years, 2/4d. The canvas tilt survived for many years and ended its life just before World War II on the back of a Birmingham baker's van. The second driver of the Daimler rigged up a small mirror so that he could see the road behind him. The company were approached by the Birmingham civic transport authorities for details, as they wanted to apply it to their own vehicles.

According to driver Reg Vincent this photograph was taken in August 1904 in Barnet - the van was being driven from London to Tipton. He is inside opening the back door. LC8242 is a 1906 number (VCC).

Ex-World War I truck used for deliveries between Tipton and Stoke.

The company replaced its Daimler with a 1904 30cwt 16hp twin cylinder Lacre (Albion) box van which cost £465. This was painted dark green with gold lettering. It had wooden wheels, low tension magneto ignition, Murray patent carburettor and governor, and ignition plugs operated by push rods from the camshaft. It had three forward and one reverse gear, and did 18 mpg. It gave excellent service for 10 years.

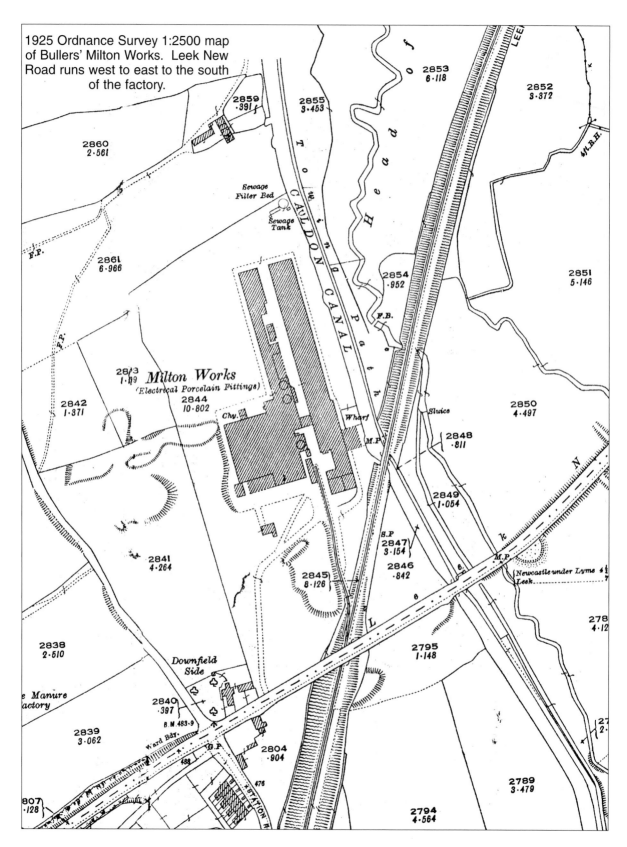

1925 Ordnance Survey 1:2500 map of Bullers' Milton Works. Leek New Road runs west to east to the south of the factory.

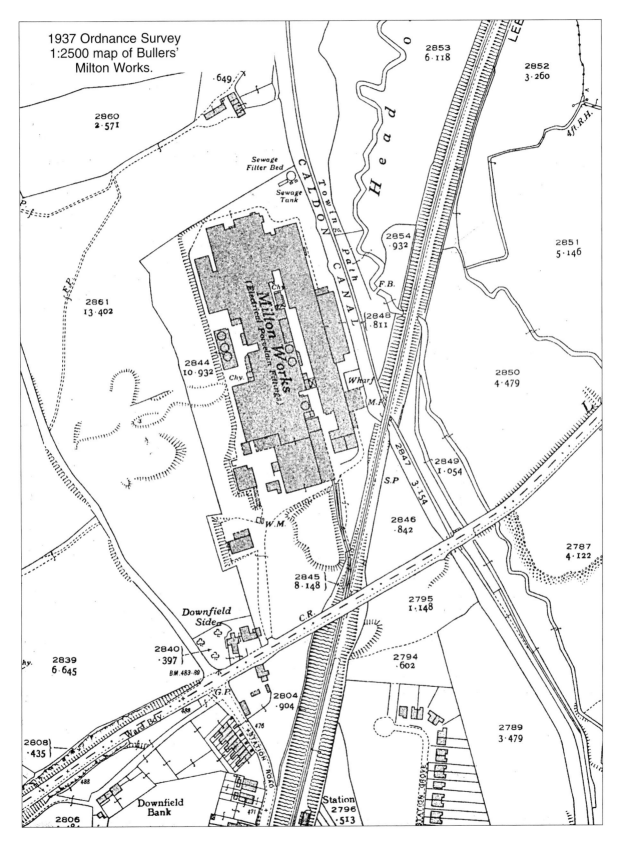

1937 Ordnance Survey 1:2500 map of Bullers' Milton Works.

Exterior view of Milton Works showing
gas fired battery stack and producers
to intermittent type hard paste kilns
c. 1925-30

Courtesy of Taylor Tunnicliff Ltd

View of Milton canal wharf showing
horses and carts moving raw materials
c. 1925-30

Courtesy of Taylor Tunnicliff Ltd

The throwing house at Hanley Works c. 1925-30.

The dressing shop at Tipton Works c. 1908

The foundry at Tipton Works c. 1908

The fitting shop at Tipton Works c. 1908.

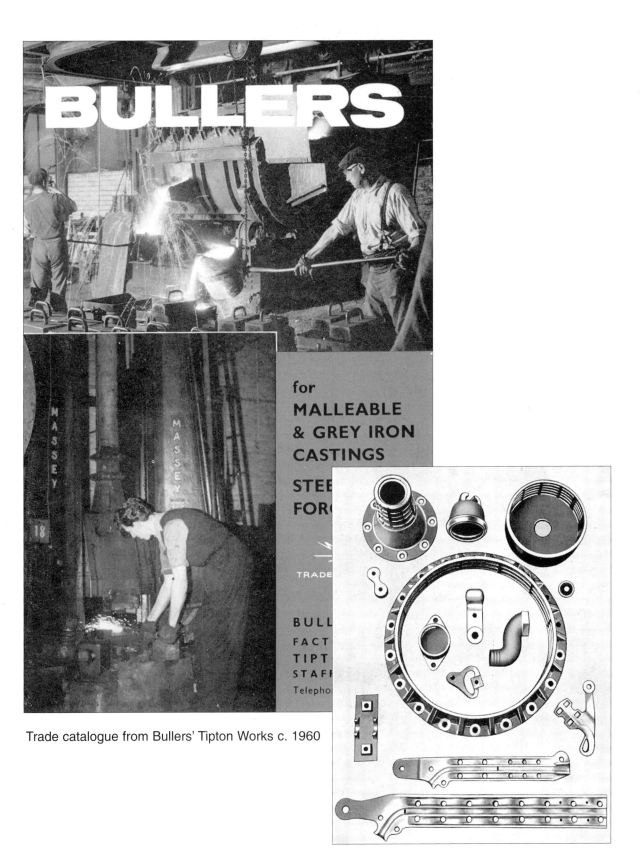

Trade catalogue from Bullers' Tipton Works c. 1960

OTHER RELATED COMPANIES

TAYLOR TUNNICLIFF

Another local company called Taylor Tunnicliff had for many years been connected with the Bullers' enterprise. They operated in neighbouring works to the Joiner's Square works at Eastwood in Hanley and manufactured a very similar range of products to that of Bullers. Eventually the two companies merged.

In 1867 an engineer named Thomas Taylor and a potter named William Tunnicliff formed a partnership and started to manufacture in a small factory called the Havelock Works in Shelton, near Hanley. Their target market was the metal manufacturers of Sheffield and Birmingham who required precision made ceramic articles. Initially therefore they manufactured items such as door furniture, handles, lamp containers, photographic developing trays, artists' palettes and hermetically sealed jars. As production levels grew they moved to Eastwood, Hanley and, when William Tunnicliff retired in 1895, a private limited company was formed with Thomas Taylor as Chairman. In 1906 Taylor's son-in-law Edward Douglas Mountford Scrivener (an architect) became a Director of the company and was later joined by Col Sir John Kent. They became joint Managing Directors.[51]

Thomas Taylor saw the future potential which the spread of electrical applications offered and turned his attention to the production of ceramic switch bases, fuse holders, mounts and insulators.

Both Bullers and Taylor Tunnicliff started production of electrical porcelain around the same time and both moved to new, larger premises outside the city. Taylor Tunnicliff relocated to Stone in 1922 and then in 1926 they acquired a second factory in Longton, (close to the current Gladstone Working Pottery Museum) where ceramic refractory components for electric fires and cookers were made. In 1928 they took over yet another factory in Hanley known as Electric and Ordnance Accessories & Co. Ltd. where small turned goods and die-pressed insulators were made. As with Bullers, a continuous programme of building and development took place throughout the life of the company.

In 1959 Bullers and Taylor Tunnicliff amalgamated and the new company become known as Allied Insulators. This merger was prompted by fear on the part of both companies that they might be the subject of a takeover bid by one of their large clients, such as BTH (British Thomson Houston) or Balfour Beatty. The key players in pushing this merger forward were John Elvine Harris for Bullers and Gerald Scrivener for Taylor Tunnicliff. This new business alliance was probably strengthened by the marriages of John Waugh Harris and John Elvine Harris to members of the Scrivener family. Prior to this merger, Taylor Tunnicliff owned three companies, Taylor Tunnicliff Refactories; Electric and Ordnance Accessories & Co Ltd and Taylor Tunnicliff Ltd, the largest of the three.

Although officially merged the companies continued to manufacture in their own premises at Stone and Milton and, to an extent, continued to compete for business. In 1981 the Stone factory was closed and production and administration were consolidated at Milton.

When the Taylor Tunnicliff office staff were relocated to Milton there appears to have been some resentment, particularly as they had been better paid than Bullers' staff. Provision had not been made for their sudden arrival and many had no desks to sit at. This did not ease their integration into the Milton establishment. Bullers' staff also reported feeling a loss of identity after this merger as new managers appeared and new or adapted ways of manufacture had to be introduced to cope with the differences between the two companies and their products.

After the merger, members of the Taylor Tunnicliff concern became the major shareholders. The products of the Tipton works were always sold to Milton, with no competition from outside. However, the Taylor Tunnicliff operation claimed that this was too expensive for them and continued to buy from other suppliers outside the company. Disputes such as this over operating practices could not have been helpful to the success of the future merged company.

ALLIED INSULATORS

Although the resources and expertise of the merged companies should have ensured continuing success for Bullers under the new name, technological, economic and world market factors caused problems for the company throughout the latter decades of the 20th century.

In 1972, with Gerald Scrivener as Chairman, it was announced in the local press that, due to the unfavourable order position of Allied Insulators, the Eastwood works of Taylor Tunnicliff at Hanley would be closed. At that time they employed 340 staff. The company by then operated four manufacturing plants - Taylor Tunnicliff at Stone (high tension porcelains); Taylor Tunnicliff at Eastwood (low tension porcelains); Taylor Tunnicliff at Longton (low tension porcelains and refractories); and Bullers at Milton (all types of electrical porcelains).[52] The Tipton plant of Bullers was still in operation at this time. A considerable proportion of the Eastwood site was sold in 1972 for £79,000[53] and it was estimated that there would be around 175 redundancies from the total workforce of 1800.

Bullers' Hanley works showing the construction of a new spray drier c. 1978.
The bottle oven is now part of a residential complex.

The company secretary at that time pointed out that, unlike the domestic pottery industry, manufacturers of electrical porcelain could not create a demand for their products - the demand had to be there and the company had to compete for these orders. This demand had been decreasing over the years as the installation of major new electrical projects slowed down. He did not believe that demand could ever rise back to previous levels. A 1978 press report blamed lack of investment by the Central Electricity Generating Board as one reason why the industry was suffering.[54]

In 1979 the company name was again changed. Many small iron foundries in the Midlands were acquired by the new Chairman Alan Lloyd. Since the manufacture of insulators now represented less than half of the Group's activities the name was changed to A.I. Industrial Products Ltd. Two main subsidiary companies were incorporated, entitled A.I. Ceramic Products Ltd. and A.I. Metal Products Ltd.[55]

They then operated under several sub-divisions which reflected the product specialisations and geographical locations of the various companies which had by then come to make up the group as follows:

- Allied Insulators High Tension Products at Milton (1500 employees)
- Allied Insulators Low Tension Products at Longton (500 employees)
- Unilator Technical Ceramics at Ruabon, Wales (250 employees)
- Advanced Materials Engineering Limited., Gateshead (30-40 employees)
- Bullers Engineering, Tipton (300 employees)
- Mason & Burns Ltd., Walsall
- Blakey's (Malleable Castings) Limited, Leeds (600 employees)[56]

The financial situation of the company continued to decline and in April 1983 the Milton workforce was reduced by 40% to only 400 employees. This was blamed on the continuing world recession and lack of demand for the industry's products.[57] This situation stood in stark contrast to the industry as it was described by Major G.A. Wade in 1926 when he stated that *"English Electrical Porcelain is today demanded all over the world in preference to any other."*[58]

In June of the same year it was announced that the Bullers Engineering plant at Tipton would close.[59] A few years later Allied Insulators High Tension Division at Milton was sold to Fairey Holdings who also owned Doulton Insulators of Tamworth.[60]

In 1985 A.I. Industrial Products changed its name to Bullers PLC. When asked why they had reverted to this name a company spokesman said *"A lot of people didn't understand the name of the company and Bullers PLC is sharp and straightforward compared with A.I."* Meanwhile Allied Insulators Low Tension Division was renamed Taylor Tunnicliff - another reversion to the previous and better known name.[61]

A 1987 restructuring within the Fairey Group slightly increased the workforce at Milton again but at the expense of their sister company Doulton Insulators at Tamworth.[62]

After these changes of ownership and restructure, the company found itself entering the 21st century as Wade Allied Holdings, having been bought out by the Beauford Group in 1999. Operations at the Milton factory had been scaled down and by the time the factory was finally closed in 2001 only about 120 skeleton staff remained on site and many of the buildings were empty or leased to other industrial concerns. The company was, by then, the only UK manufacturer of porcelain disc insulators.

Aerial view of the Tipton Works c. 1930-40.

REFERENCES

1. GENUKI UK and Ireland Genealogy. www.cs.ncl.ac.uk/genuki/DEV/Whimple
2. www.mortimer.co.uk/manors/cliston.htm
3. Devon Record Office, Exeter. Buller documents 2065M/F6/10
4. Tithe maps of Wales at the National Library of Wales. www.llgc.org.uk/dm/dm0030.htm
5. Mortimer. Op. cit.
6. Buller, Thomas Wentworth. UK patent no. 12599. Improvements in the manufacture of earthenware.1849
7. Infringement of a patent. Ford v. Buller in Staffordshire Advertiser 27th June 1851 p.3
8. Devon Record Office document DRO D1508M/Mining/26
9. Letter from Bullers Ltd. to The Registrar of Joint Stock Companies 27th September 1895
10. Jewitt, Llewellyn. *The Ceramic Art of Great Britain*. New edition. Orchard Editions, 1985 p. 204
10A. Billings Devonshire Directory 1857.
11. Buller. Op. cit.
12. Jewitt. Op. cit.
12A. Great Exhibition of the Works of Industries of All Nations 1851. Official Descriptive and Illustrated Catalogue
     Vol 1. London Clowes and Sons 1851 p 128.
13. Infringement of a patent. Op. cit.
13A. Devon Record Office, Exeter. Will of Thomas Wentworth Buller of Strete Ralegh 1852. Buller documents 48/22/21.

14. Billings Devonshire Directory 1857.
15. Devon Record Office, Exeter. Buller documents 4622M/T18.
16. Letter 27th September 1895. Op. cit.
16A. Devon Record Office, Exeter. Buller documents 4622M/T18.
17. Buller, Wentworth W. & Mugford, Jabez Hearn. UK patent no. 3194. Improvements in spur supporting rings for fixing plates, dishes and other like articles in glost ovens. 1862
18. *Jones's Mercantile Directory of the Pottery District of Staffordshire* 1864. London, 1864. p.62
19. Devon Record Office, Exeter. Buller documents 2065M/F6/3
20. Huntbach, Alfred. *Hanley: Stoke-on-Trent* 1910 p.38
21. Powell, Geoffrey. *Buller: a Scapegoat? A life of General Sir Redvers Buller 1839-1908.* Leo Cooper, 1994. p.5
22. J.G. Harrod & Co. *Postal and Commercial Directory of Staffordshire 1870.* p.874.
23. *Kelly's Directory Birmingham 1876*
24. *Kelly's Directory Staffordshire 1884.* p.538
25. The manufacture of porcelain insulators in *The Engineer* 12th June 1931 p.658-9
26. Devon Record Office. Exeter. Buller documents 2065M F6/3
27. Memorandum of Association. Buller Jobson & Co. Ltd. 8th June 1885
28. 1881 British Population Census
29. *Keates's Gazetteer and Directory of the Staffordshire Potteries: Newcastle and District 1889-90.* p.219
30. Memorandum of Association. Bullers Limited. 6th October 1880
31. Letter 27th September 1895. Op. cit.
32. Memorandum of Association 1885. Op. Cit.
33. Harris, Nigel. *The Yarlet Story.* 1993.
34. The manufacture of insulators in *Electrical Power* March 1905 p.49-53
35. Obituary of John Waugh Harris in *Pottery Gazette and Glass Trades Review* 1st March 1920 p.377
36. Obituary of Ralph Guy Harris in *Journal of the British Ceramic Society* October 1963 p.104
37. Greene, John. *Brightening the long days: hospital tile pictures.* Tiles & Architectural Ceramics Soc, 1987. p.58
38. Pennell, Isaac and Harris, John Thomas. UK patent no. 10817. Improved apparatus or appliance for use in supporting ceramic- ware in enamel-kilns whilst being fired. 1891
39. Hackley, Edward John and Pennell, Frank Reed. UK patent no. 236687. Improvements in apparatus for pugging or extruding plastic potter's clay and the like. 1925
40. Memorandum of Association 1890. Op. cit.
41. The manufacture of insulators in *Electrical Power* March 1905 p.49-53
42. Chambers, Edward John. UK patent no. 2373. Improvements in the socket joints of metallic telegraph poles and UK patent no. 11544 Improvements in the manufacture of the insulator arms of telegraph poles and poles for carrying conductors of electricity generally. 1895
43. Harris, Nigel. Op. cit.
44. Hargreaves, Thomas. Map of the Staffordshire Potteries and Newcastle. 1832.
45. Memorandum of Association. 1885. Op. cit.
46. Jewitt. Op. cit.
47. Bullers Limited. Undated catalogue.
48. British electro-technical pottery in *Financial Times* 16th July 1930
49. Ibid.
50. Fernie, K. & Price, E.E. Bullers change to butane in *Ceramics* November 1969 p.14-22
51. Taylor Tunnicliff in *A British Bulletin of Commerce Survey* November 1954
52. Two North Staffs insulator factories to be merged in *The Sentinel* 5th May 1972
53. Take-over bid rejected by shareholders in *The Sentinel* 29th December 1972
54. New technology brings in orders in *The Sentinel* 17th February 1978
55. North Staffs company to change name? in *The Sentinel* 2nd February 1979
56. Allied Insulators. Company brochure. c.1980
57. Axe to fall on 150 jobs in *The Sentinel* 21st April 1983
58. Wade, G.A. Manufacture of electrical porcelain in *Cox's Pottery and Glass Trade Year Book* 1926 p.85
59. Another A.I. plant to close down in *The Sentinel* 28th June 1983
60. A.I. firm sold for £2.5m in *The Sentinel* 21st February 1986
61. Bright outlook for city firm in *The Sentinel* 9th April 1985
62. Jobs boost for Milton firm in *The Sentinel* 16th June 1987

Presses in the sliphouse at Milton 2001.

Extruded clay emerging from the pug mill at Milton 2001.

Below: Bushings at Milton 2001.

Dipping of insulators at Milton 2001.

Shaping the top of an insulator to enable fitting of metal cap Milton 2001.

Hot pressing of insulators at Milton 2001.

Canal and railway links at Milton, 1999.

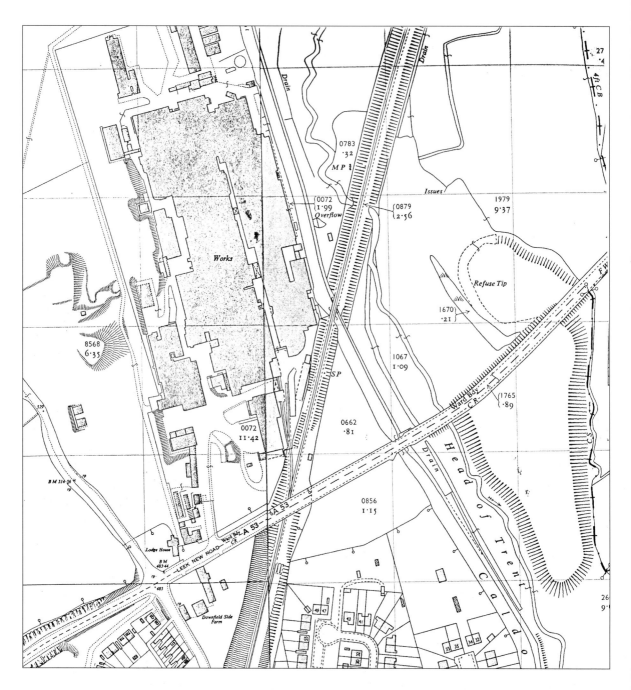

1961 Ordnance Survey 1:2500 map of Bullers' Milton Works.

Chapter 2

BULLERS INDUSTRIAL PRODUCTS: EARLY PRODUCTS

KILN FURNITURE AND ASSOCIATED PRODUCTS

Thomas Wentworth Buller's original business was located in Bovey Tracey in Devon where he was in partnership with his brother-in-law John Divitt. The company there appears to have concentrated on the manufacture of earthenware items. One of their main products was a range of what we now call kiln furniture - small earthenware devices for supporting and separating pottery ware during the firing process. A lucrative market existed for such items amongst the Staffordshire potteries. In 1850 Mr. James Mayer, of Thomas, John and Joseph Mayer of Burslem, stated that his company used about 40,000 gross cockspurs (a type of kiln furniture) in one year.[1]

The manufacturers of such spurs and stilts are described in Scarratt's 1906 book *Old Times in the Potteries*. It recounts that in 1846 a Mr Charles Ford took out a patent for spur and stilt manufacture (3 years before Thomas Buller) noting that until this time each pottery had made their own kiln furniture manually, but now that machinery was available to carry out this operation, the items were being more commonly bought in. He said: *"Messrs. Bullers Ltd., commenced some years afterwards, also a number of others, so that now few, if any, make their own stilts and spurs."* The automation of the process ensured a more uniform product which reduced losses in the firing.[2]

The aforementioned Charles Ford, an engineer from Shelton, challenged Buller's right to manufacture similar goods to his own in a similar manner and issued two warnings in 1849 and 1851 to other pottery manufacturers against copying his invention. In advertisements in the Staffordshire Advertiser he threatened to *"stop the use thereof, and also take proceedings against the maker."*[3] Ford's patent was entitled *'Improvements in the manufacture of pottery or earthenware and in the tools, instruments, or apparatus employed therein, part or parts of which improvements are applicable to other similar purposes.'*[4] The patent applied to the manufacture of small pots, ink stands, door knobs and other furniture ornaments and to cockspurs, stilts and pins, all of which were also being made by Buller.

Ford brought an action against Thomas Wentworth Buller in Her Majesty's Court of Queen's Bench at Westminster, accusing him of manufacturing and selling cockspurs using his patented method. The case was heard at the assizes of the County of Stafford in 1850 and Ford lost the case.[5] The reason for his defeat was that the claims of his original patent were too extensive as they included *"any and every pressing and stamping apparatus,"* which would have included methods already in use by others. Ford therefore had to reissue his patent with a disclaimer in 1851 saying *"I further state that the manufacture of cockspurs is the chief and most valuable part of my said Invention, and I am desirous of not risking my title thereto by claiming anything else."*[6]

Buller had registered his first patent prior to this, on the 3rd November 1849, and it was entitled *"Improvements in the Manufacture of Earthenware"*.[7] It is an unusual patent in that it did not concentrate on one product or process but covered a seemingly wide range of items, just as Charles Ford's had done.

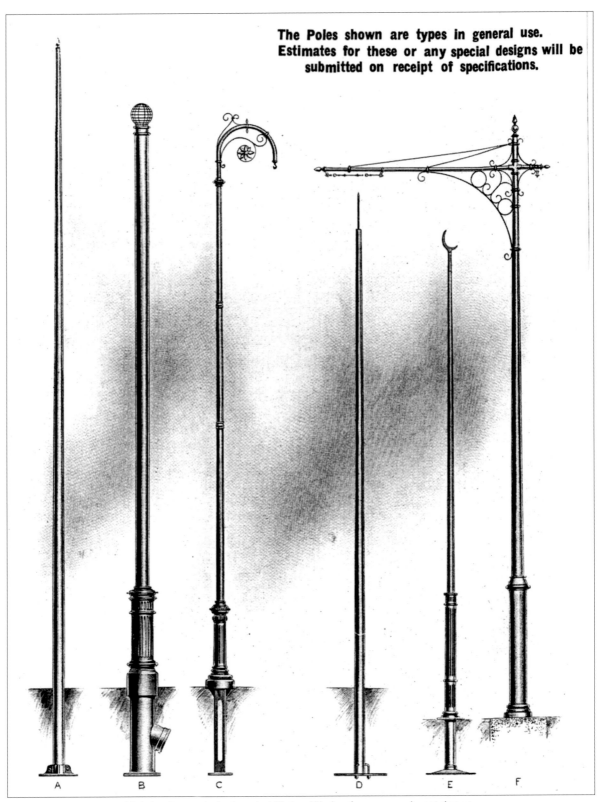

The Poles shown are types in general use. Estimates for these or any special designs will be submitted on receipt of specifications.

A   B   C   D   E   F

Metal poles manufactured at Tipton Works, from an early catalogue.

Its first claim was for an improvement in the mode of manufacturing kiln furniture known as 'cockspurs' and 'pins' used to separate items during the firing process. It also registered an improved method for the manufacture of jelly cans or other similar ware, an improved method of manufacturing toy tea cups; and lastly a method of ornamenting moulded or pressed articles by impressing upon them an engraved pattern or design.

It is interesting to examine the first item in the patent [see illustration below] as the process appears to have been transferred by the company to its new premises in Hanley. Buller invented a set of dies which produced 'cockspurs' in the form of a grid of equilateral triangles. This allowed greater economy in the use of clay, with little wastage, and the final products were of a lower height than previously, thus allowing more wares to be packed into the kiln saggars for firing. The filled dies were put into a fly-wheel press to effect their production and then taken to a drying room. The same method was described in the patent for production of the pins which were inserted into the sides of saggars to support plates during firing without leaving any marks on the plate surface.

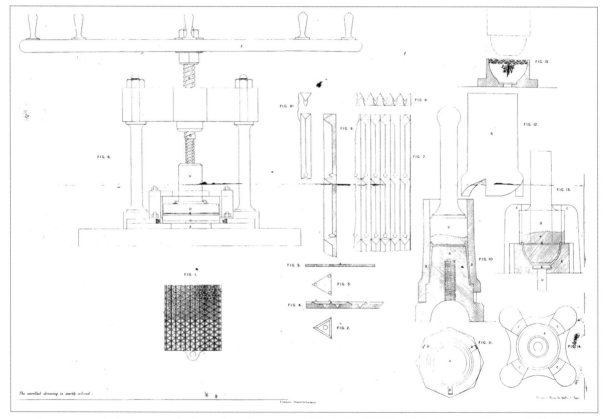

Improvements in the manufacture of earthenware. Patent No. 12599, 1849, Thomas Wentworth Buller.

The part of the patent referring to jelly can production involved the pressing of clay into a double skinned mould by use of a plunger and mallet. A similar process was described for the toy cup process. The last patented process involved pressing an item whilst the clay was still in its 'green' or soft state into a die which had an engraved and inked pattern cut into it. Some archaeological evidence has been found in Devon of the products in this patent.

In 1862 Wentworth William Buller (Thomas Wentworth's son) patented another design, with Jabez Hearn Mugford, for spur supporting rings for fixing plates and dishes in glost ovens.[8] Their address for the patent is given as Bovey Tracey but, as by this time the business was also operating in Hanley, they would have been guaranteed a large local market there.

By 1891 the partnership with John T. Harris had been in existence for eight years and he was now also involved in the quest for new and improved ways of manufacturing kiln furniture. With Isaac Pennell (described in the patent as Potter's Manager), John Harris (Earthenware Manufacturer) created a new apparatus for stacking earthenware or china whilst being fired.[9] Its design is not dissimilar to equipment still in use today and was to provide a more stable structure to hold dishes in place by attaching pillars of supporting 'thimbles' to a metal base. The benefits were to allow easier transfer from workbench to kiln; to decrease the amount of marks on the ware; and to fit more pieces into the kiln.

From this date onwards there do not appear to have been any substantial developments within Bullers of these types of products

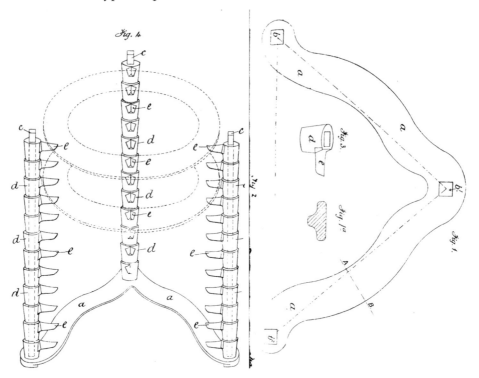

Improved apparatus for supporting ceramic ware in enamel kilns.... Patent No. 10817, 1891, Isaac Pennell and John T. Harris.

OTHER EARLY PRODUCTS

Details of the other products manufactured in the late 19th and early 20th centuries can be found in patents, trade directories, company advertisements and in the pattern books of the company. From around 1892 onwards the majority of patents relate to insulators or to their poles and fixings. The pattern books provide some additional technical and commercial information which give us a more detailed background about the company's activities.

Courtesy of Taylor Tunnicliff Ltd

Plates supported by kiln furniture during the firing process.

BELOW: Kiln furniture designed by Isaac Pennell and John Thomas Harris in 1891.

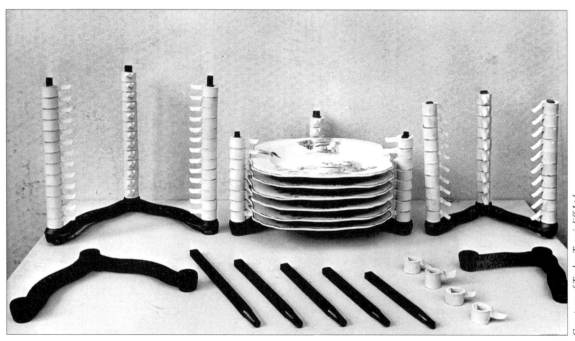

Courtesy of Taylor Tunnicliff Ltd

As earthenware was the body with which the company was familiar it would be reasonable to assume that use of this was continued after the move north in 1860. As their range of products was extended, so the range of clay bodies used grew, and by the end of the 19th century these included: mortar clay, insulator clay, ivory or granite clay, red furniture clay, black furniture clay, brown insulator clay.

It is not clear at what point in time the use of porcelain was introduced although it is specifically mentioned in pattern books dating from around 1890.

The following items are listed in an early pattern book. Where indicated, the type of clay used is shown.

Mullers (a flat tool for grinding on a slab)
Grinding pans
Pestles (either all porcelain or with wooden handle set into porcelain base)
"Pot eyes"
Cistern pull handles
Waste pipes and overflows
Bedstead spindles (made of granite clay)
Organ stops (made of ivory clay)
Handles (with note "To be always marked Rd.No. 517737 [1907]")
Lever knobs (Black figures granite clay - blue figures black furniture clay)
Mortice roses
Lacquer pots (made of special insulator clay)
Balls
Drinking fountain nozzles
Inkwells (made of insulator clay)
Perambulator handles

This is a small sample taken from just one pattern book.

Between 1870 and 1884 Ernest Wentworth Buller filed several patents all concerned with improving the methods of attaching door knobs and handles to their spindles, to prevent them from coming loose with continued use, for example. These are listed in Appendix 2. Another patent relates to what it describes as *"the terminal ornaments of metallic furniture"* such as bed knobs.[10] The 1886 pattern book describes these as *"cage spires and mounts"*. A wide range of door furniture such as knobs, finger plates, and keyhole surrounds was manufactured for many years - indeed until the 1960s - and in the early days was probably one of the main product ranges. The fact that the company patented these designs, and noted in the pattern book that they must be marked with the design registration number, indicates the commercial importance attached to these items. Early pieces seem to have remained undecorated but could have been supplied to other Staffordshire companies for painting. Later 20th century door sets were painted by Bullers' staff in the Joiner's Square and Tipton factories or had lithographic printed decoration applied.

The cost of finger plates in 1886 was 1s 2^1/$_2$d per dozen. Number plates were also available at 3s 8^3/$_4$d per dozen with an additional charge of 4s 6d if they were to be printed.

In 1885 eighteen different sizes of pestles and mortars were available for purchase. The

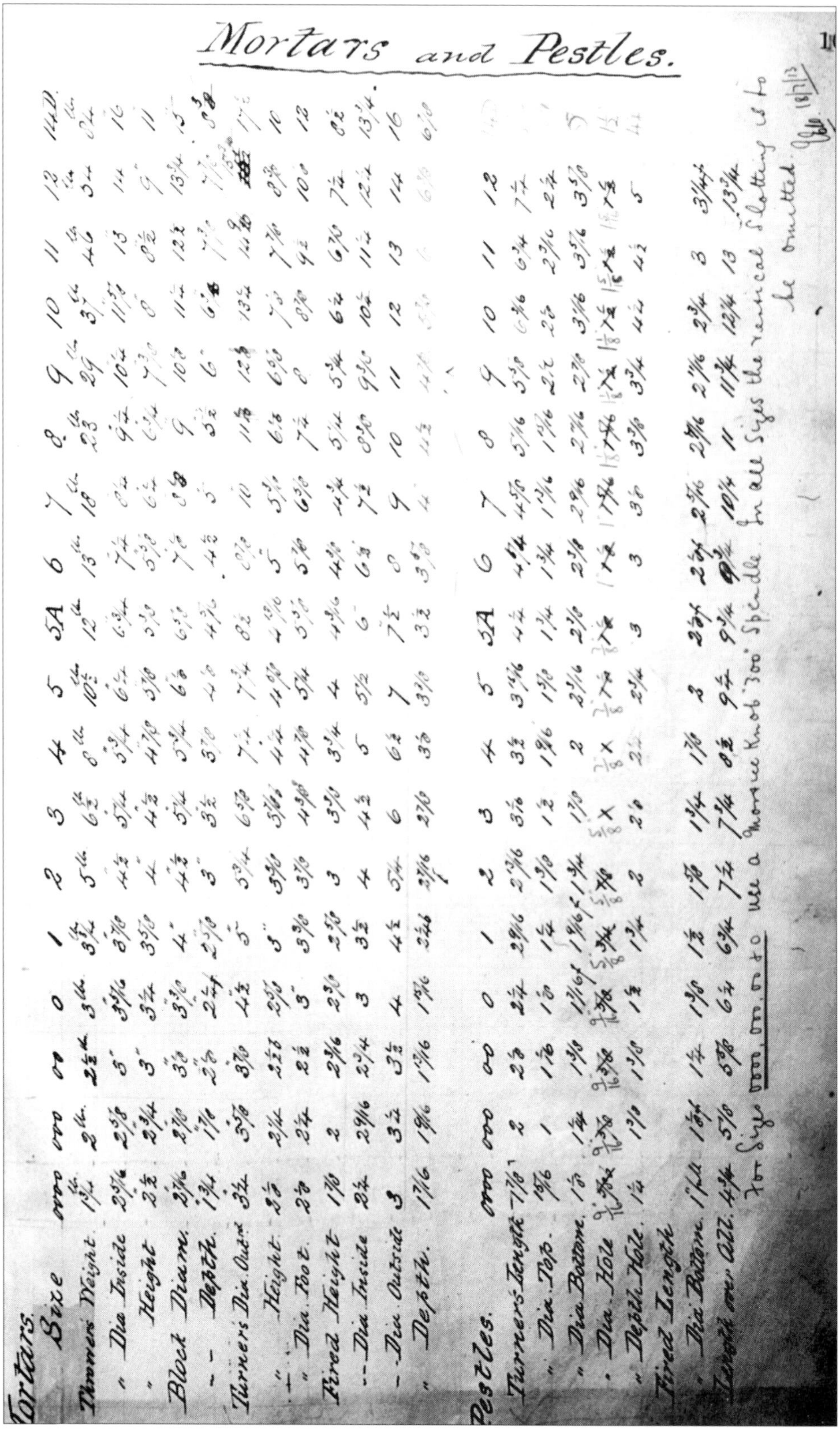

Mortars and Pestles.

(handwritten size chart — Mortars and Pestles, with columns of measurements)

Size chart for the range of mortars and pestles produced in the late 19th century.

Courtesy of Allied Insulators Ltd.

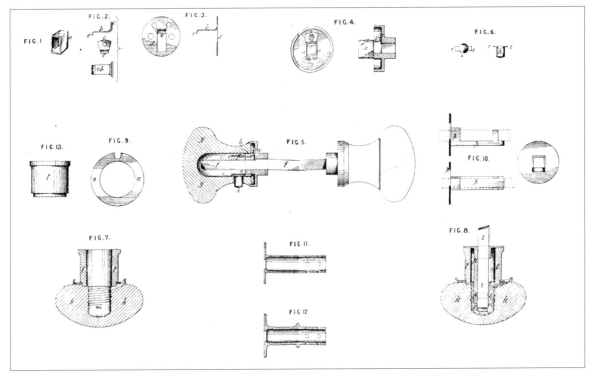

Improvements in knobs and in their attachment to spindles. Patent No.5184 1881 Ernest W. Buller.

cost of these ranged from 2s 2d per dozen for the smallest up to 60s per dozen for the largest.

The names of company customers in the pattern books indicate which industries were being supplied. [see Appendix 3] By the 1890s the production of electrical accessories for domestic use had become an important source of business. Wall plugs, ceiling roses, fuse boxes, cut outs and lamp plugs were being designed and produced for companies as far afield as Paiste H. J. of New York and Hartvigson for a project in Russia. From the descriptions in the pattern book it would appear that one or two of these items were designed in the London Office and the drawings then sent to Hanley for manufacture.

Contracts with the sanitary ware industry included with Twyfords Ltd. for whom Bullers produced *"Twyfords Waste and Standing Overflow"*, with Howsons, who were a neighbouring company in Eastwood, and with T. & R. Boote, who ordered an outlet and slide cover. The Dental Manufacturing Company ordered pestles; Keeling and Walker ordered sparking plugs and Selas Lighting bought lampshades.

Other pottery manufacturers purchased porcelain components from Bullers for their mechanical equipment, such as pump rams. At the turn of the century, these included Stoke-on-Trent companies J. & G. Meakin, Johnson Brothers, Bishop & Stonier and the Old Hall Porcelain Works, whilst the Scottish pottery industry was represented by R. Cochrane & Co. of the Britannia Pottery, Glasgow, J. & M. P. Bell & Co. of the Glasgow Pottery and D. Methven & Sons of the Kirkcaldy Pottery.

Although a range of porcelain items such as those mentioned above continued to be designed and manufactured by the company, by far the bulk of the late 19th and 20th century production was dedicated to the production of electrical porcelain insulators.

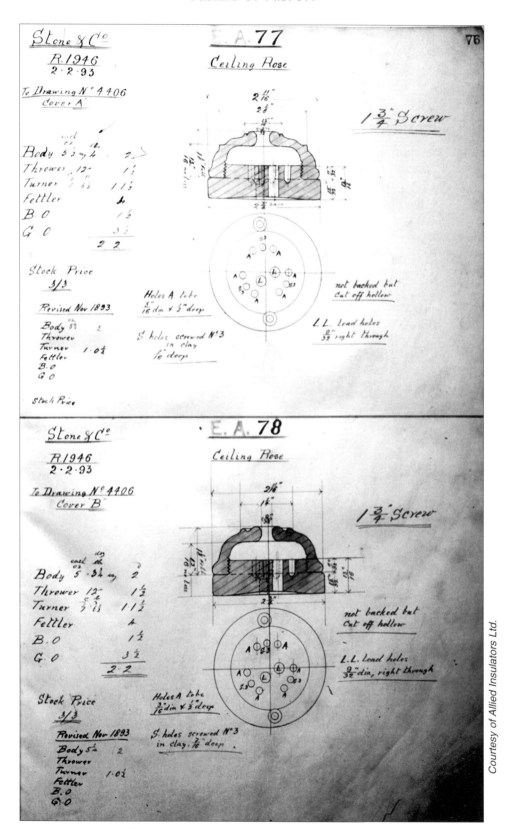

Drawings 1893 for ceiling roses for Stone & Co.

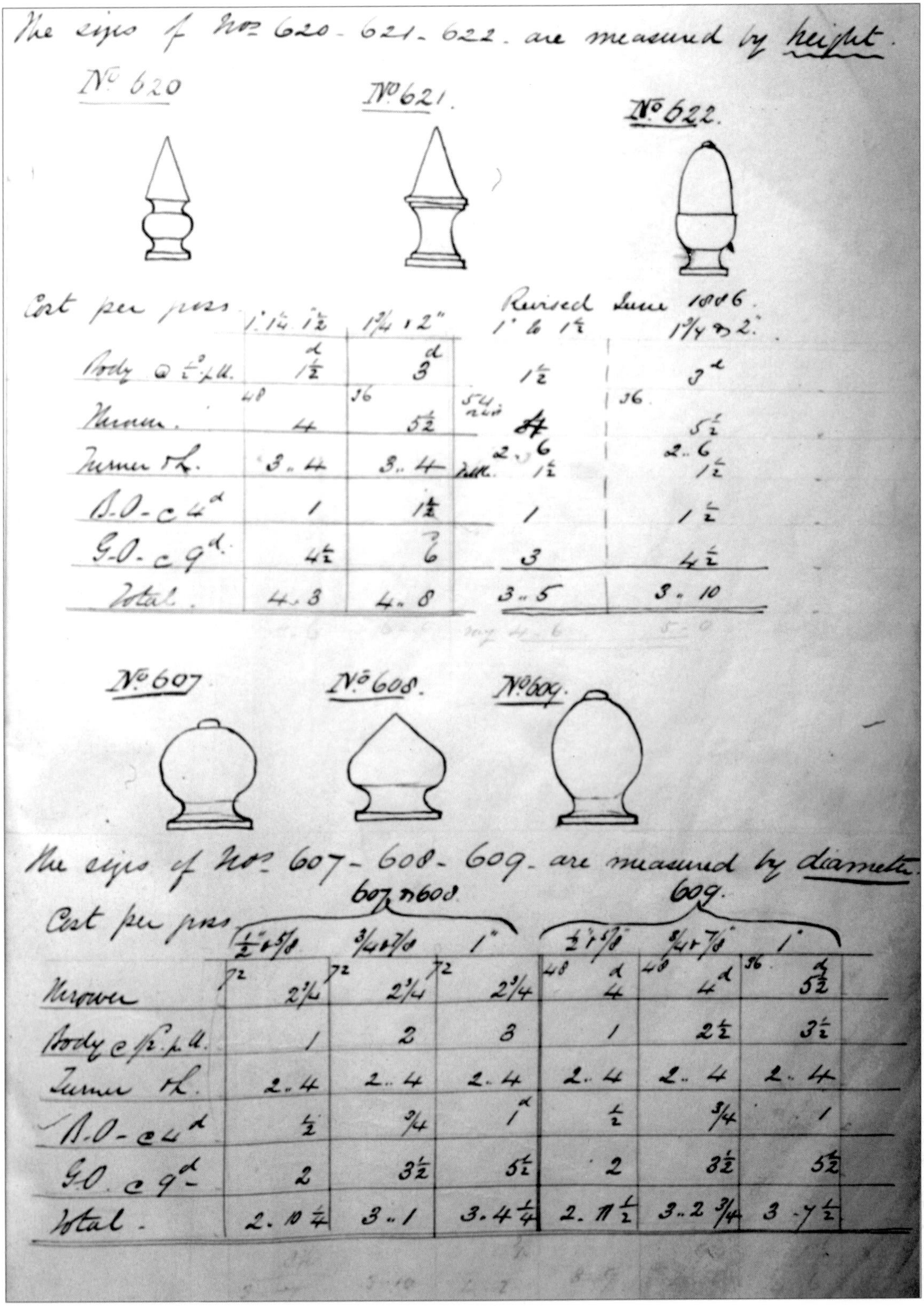

The sizes of Nos 620 - 621 - 622 - are measured by height.

No 620 — No 621. — No 622.

Cost per gross	1", 1¼, 1½	1¾ & 2"	Revised June 1886. 1" to 1½	1¾ & 2"
Body @ ½d per lb.	1½d	3d	1½	3d
Thrower.	48 4	36 5½	54 4	36 5½
Turner & L.	3..4	3..4	2..6 1½	2..6 1½
B.O. @ 4d	1	1½	1	1½
G.O. @ 9d.	4½	6	3	4½
Total.	4..3	4..8	3..5	3..10

No 607 — No 608. — No 609.

The sizes of Nos 607 - 608 - 609 - are measured by diameter.

Cost per gross	607 & 608: ½" & 5/8	607 & 608: ¾ & 7/8	607 & 608: 1"	609: ½ & 5/8	609: ¾ & 7/8	609: 1"
Thrower	72 2¼	72 2¼	72 2¼	48 4d	48 4d	36 5½d
Body @ ½ per lb.	1	2	3	1	2½	3½
Turner & L.	2..4	2..4	2..4	2..4	2..4	2..4
B.O. @ 4d	½	¾	1d	½	¾	1
G.O. @ 9d	2	3½	5½	2	3½	5½
Total.	2..10¼	3..1	3..4¼	2..11½	3..2¾	3..7½

Courtesy of Allied Insulators Ltd.

Cage spires and mounts for bedsteads and similar furnishings c. 1885 showing manufacturing costs per gross

BULLERS' FIRING TRIAL RINGS *"The best medium for controlling the heat treatment for ceramics"*[11]

Bullers' Rings were first mass produced by Bullers around 1910 and their use soon became widespread throughout the pottery industry. They are annular rings made by pressing together a blend of ceramic materials and fluxes but these remain unfired before use. By using these rings it is possible to monitor and control the firing process without depending on visual inspection. Most ceramic bodies initially expand during heating but start to shrink after 900 degrees centigrade. The rings are placed amongst the ware within the kiln in specially designed prefired stands. They are then removed periodically through openings in the kiln wall and allowed to cool. Their shrinkage is measured as a percentage of the original size by placing the ring in a special guage.

This principle of measuring the firing shrinkage of ceramic samples was used as early as 1782 by Josiah Wedgwood and examples of his pyrometer and cylinders, along with the later, more sophisticated Bullers versions, can be seen in the Potteries Museum & Art Gallery in Stoke-on-Trent. There seems to be no evidence that Bullers invented such rings - there is no patent under their name for such a product - it seems that the Buller name was attached to the product by default.

At the Taylor Tunnicliff factory in Longton, Bullers' rings were manufactured by hand pressing until the 1980s after which time spray dried materials and autopressing were introduced providing greater consistency in the product and faster production times. Four types of rings are manufactured for use in various temperature ranges covering stoneware, bricks and tiles; porcelain and refractory items; low temperature materials such as earthenwares and hard porcelain. They can be used in both intermittent and tunnel kilns.

A 1967 advertisement gives the contact address for information on the product as Bullers Limited, Joiners Square Works, Hanley. The manufacture of Bullers' rings is currently (2002) carried out by Taylor Tunnicliff in their Longton factory.[12]

Bullers' firing trial rings placed in intermittent kiln.

Bullers' firing trial rings placed in a saggar.
An opening has been left for their periodic removal.

Removing a Bullers' ring from intermittent kiln.

Removing a Bullers' ring during firing of intermittent kiln.

Evelyn Winter manufacturing Bullers'
firing trial rings in the 1950s at
Hanley Works,

Barbara Maddox manufacturing Bullers'
firing trial rings at Hanley works in the
1970s. (Guards have now been added.)

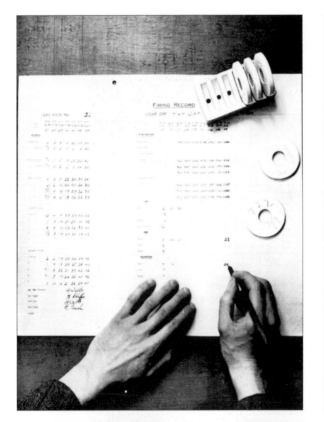

Taking readings on the special guage and logging the results during the firing process.

Eric Bentley and Joan Adkins testing and logging rings, 1970s.

INSULATORS

Background

The development of insulators followed the spread of the railways and the electric telegraph system in the 19th century, the electrical telegraph having been first patented in 1837 by William F. Cooke and Charles Wheatstone. The function of insulators is to support conductors and hold them in safe and correct positions whilst withstanding the effects of weather and other mechanical forces. Early insulators were made of organic materials such as tarred felt or goose quills. Not surprisingly these materials proved unsuccessful as they have a short lifespan and little resistance to the elements. Many other interesting and unusual designs were produced during the early and mid 19th century both in Europe and North America.

North America initially favoured wooden insulators and fixings as they had a large supply of timber readily available. They were used in telegraphic applications and on San Francisco trolley bus lines and some were apparently still in use as recently as the mid 1980s. Some varieties of British wooden insulators had rubber linings to increase their insulating properties and insulators made entirely from rubber and other composite materials such as ebonite and vulcanite were also developed both in Europe and America.

Early American insulators were wedged down onto tapered wooden pins with tar, and by the 1860s threaded insulators on threaded wooden pins were found. Early European insulators were also unthreaded and cemented onto steel pins rather than wooden ones. An 1886 Buller design for a German client specified the use of varnished hemp in the bolt hole to adhere to the fitting. The use of metal pins allowed the development of more compact insulators in this country - the American ones had to be wider to accommodate the wooden pin. The practice of cementing in Britain, rather than screwing on, led to a lack of standardisation in design of pin holes. To cope with this problem, many of Bullers' designs offered the client the choice of screwed, corrugated or plain bolt holes, an order for John C. Fuller & Son of Bow for a T223 insulator being an example. The corrugated hole was made with the same tools as used for making pestles - a borer and corrugator.

The next development was the manufacture of glass and other ceramic insulators. These were found to possess better insulating properties and to be able to withstand the weather. They were not, of course, impervious to attack from stone throwers (vandalism appears to have been a problem even in those early times!) and so companies such as Bullers developed an iron cladding to fit over the insulator as protection. This design improvement caused problems of its own as insects such as spiders used the cavity it provided as shelter in which to nest, thus hampering efficiency.

In America the earliest porcelain insulators date from around 1885 and they were mainly used in power applications rather than in telegraphy. In England, stoneware was used from the mid 1840s with companies such as Stiff's and Doulton's in Lambeth adding insulators to their range of saltglazed stoneware productions and Joseph Bourne of Denby in Derbyshire producing them from around 1860. Most published accounts give 1868 as the date from which Bullers began to manufacture insulators and company records include drawings from around 1875 onwards.

It is believed that a porcelain body was first used in Staffordshire around 1887-88[13] but an engineer named Ernest Watkin, writing in 1924 reported that difficulties had been experienced

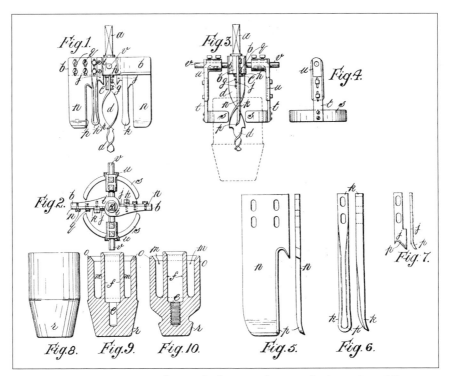

Improvements in means for use in the manufacture of telegraph and like insulators. Patent 3798 1909 George W. Carr

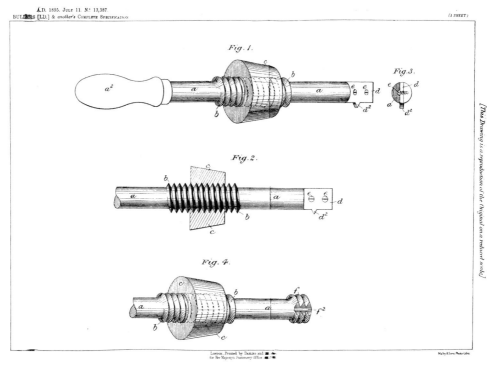

A new or improved tool or appliance for cutting screw threads in hollow articles of clay or other soft materials. Patent No 13387, 1895, John Thomas Harris.

in the early days in the development of high quality porcelain. This had occasionally led to breakdowns and had for a time undermined the electrical engineers' faith in porcelain insulators.[14]

Manufacture

The main ingredients of the electrical porcelain body are ball clay, china clay, felspar and quartz. These were obtained from Dorset, Cornwall and Norway. The choice of porcelain as a preferred medium was due to its ability to retain its electrical and mechanical properties when exposed both to the weather and to the electrical discharges which occur on the surface in moist or polluted environments, and to its durability.

As with most companies in the pottery industry, the recipes for the composition of the clay body were kept secret. A 1926 article notes that *"the various firms engaged in insulator manufacture maintain a profound secrecy about all concerning the 'sliphouse'"* [15] In recent years, 40-50% clay, 35%-45% quartz and 15-20% felspar were the usual proportions. However, when Bullers first manufactured insulators it is likely that flint would have been used instead of quartz and the Joiner's Square factory was conveniently located close to flint mills on the Caldon Canal. A technical article published in 1905 noted that the company did not obtain their clays for porcelain locally, reserving the use of local clays for saggar manufacture.[16]

Two company engineers (by then Allied Insulators) writing in 1974 commented that insulator bodies had changed little as regards their clay content, but that manufacturers could now take advantage of the consistent, blended clays which were commercially available.[17] Latterly, the company used two bodies - a standard body and a high strength body which had a higher alumina content and was used where there was a likelihood of higher mechanical stresses (e.g. earthquakes) or vandalism.

The methods used in preparing the body and its conversion into the finished product differed little from other branches of the pottery industry. In the sliphouse at Milton which backed onto the canal, clays for larger insulators were blended in the usual wet process, whilst for the smaller porcelain products (such as light switches, or electric fires) the clay, instead of being worked in the plastic state, was dried, ground up into a powder and slightly moistened before being pressed in steel dies, usually by female workers. In the wet process, raw materials such as felspar and quartz were finely crushed before being mixed with the clay and water to form slip. Electromagnets and sieves removed any impurities before the mixture was pressed between cloths to remove excess moisture and produce slabs of clay. These were then further worked by hand or by the pug machines to remove air and ensure a well blended clay. The company made use of many German technologies during the inter-war years, and the pug machines at Milton were an example of this.

Depending on the type of insulator being made, it was thrown and turned; cast; jolleyed or die pressed. As technology advanced, the throwers ceased to be required, their work being taken over by more automated processes. A 1913 publication extolled the virtue of thrown insulators noting that they were superior to *"cheaper foreign made ones which are not 'thrown' on the potter's wheel, and which are imported here, and even exported again to our colonies, and in some cases certified as English made."*[18] As with other areas of pottery manufacture the thrower was a man and his assistant frequently a female operative. Staff in the turning shop were also both male and female. As there was no equal pay legislation for most of the 20th century, it was cheaper to employ women where they were equally capable of carrying out the work.

Jolleying and turning were still in operation until the factory closed. The clay body for jolleying could be used directly from the pug mill whilst patterns which were shaped by turning had to be allowed to dry slightly until they were 'leather hard', having by then lost around 16%-17% of their moisture.

The jolleying process involved a mould of plaster of Paris shaped internally to reproduce the outer profile of the insulator. Clay was placed into this mould and, whilst the mould was rotating, the operative used a profile tool to shape the internal dimensions. The plaster mould absorbed some of the moisture from the clay allowing the insulator to be removed without damage.

A tool shop was maintained on-site to manufacture and set up the profile guages and forms required for turning these blanks into shaped insulators. A 1926 article noted that all the insulator factories had such departments and remarked upon the high degree of skill found in them. *"Much care and thought is lavished on the design of the tools, some of them being extraordinarily complex, producing in one movement insulators having in some cases hundreds of holes in them, and it is not unusual for a manufacturer to be called upon to make a porcelain having holes through in various directions, very thin walls, several undercuts, and one or two threads and tapped holes."* [19]

Considerable care had to be taken in the drying and firing of insulators as any cracks or blemishes, tolerable or concealable in other branches of the pottery industry, would cause the insulator to break down under electrical test. Electrical porcelain was normally fired to a higher temperature than other wares to ensure complete vitrosity of the body itself. Insulators produced by both the wet and dry processes were glazed.

Glazes have always played a particularly important role in the quality of an insulator. They add mechanical strength to the body as well as giving the more obvious protective shield against the weather, pollution and electrical discharges. In more recent times, semiconducting glazes have been used to control voltage stresses on the insulator surface. The glaze enabled the surface to be easily cleaned by rain under normal conditions or manually in dirty environments and this was a job carried out regularly by Post Office operatives when cities and towns suffered from the pollution of soot and other effluents. In the 1930s the Post Office experimented with unglazed insulators and reported that their performance was surprisingly good.[20]

An 1897 pattern for a component for the

Thrower and his assistant Hanley Works c. 1908.

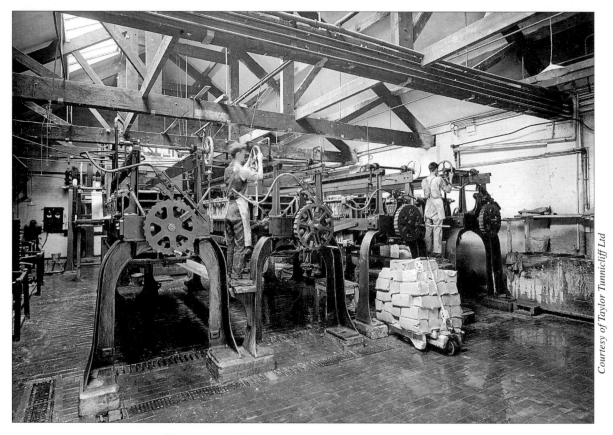

Courtesy of Taylor Tunnicliff Ltd

Sliphouse at Milton showing filter presses c. 1925-30.

Standard Wire Co. showed two prices in the pattern book depending on whether the item was purchased in the biscuit or glazed state. The cost is in code so we cannot tell what the actual difference was - Stock price y/- gross biscuit and Dt/x gross glazed - or for what purpose the two different types might have been required.

The final stage in the manufacture of insulators, as with other pottery, was the firing of the ware. A range of kilns was always in use at Milton, ranging from the early bottle ovens fired by coal to a selection of more modern electric and gas-fired kilns of varying sizes and designs, both continuous tunnel for the smaller pieces and intermittent for the larger insulators. Kilns were fired every day - evidence of the amount of work being carried out at the factory - only being shut down for the Potters' Week holidays. The kiln men were highly respected for their skills and intuition learned over many years of working in their particular specialism. The financial success of the company depended to a large extent on their abilities. Dedication to their kilns required them to be present throughout firings, breaking off from leisure time to return to the factory to check readings and issue instructions as the firing progressed.

The smaller wares were fired in the intermittent kilns in saggars, in the spaces around the larger pieces and a saggar maker was employed on the works until the 1980s. By that time there were no apprentice saggar makers and so saggars were bought in as required.

Although the older bottle ovens, intermittent and continuous tunnel kilns, have at various times been used in all branches of the pottery industry, large insulators known as bushings or, colloquially, shedders, required a special design of large kiln to accommodate them. These large insulators were built by a process known as 'sticking up'. Jolleyed sections were assembled vertically, being stuck together with slip by skilled operatives on ladders and lifts to raise them high above the factory floor as the insulator grew in size. The completed bushings were aerographed with glaze and wheeled into their own special kilns for firing. These kilns took 4 days to be fired up to 1205 degrees and then 4 days to cool. The tunnel kiln firing ranges between 1190 and 1220 degrees, with 1205 considered the optimum.

After firing, insulators had to be tested to ensure that they were free from defects and safe to use. All high voltage insulators would undergo such tests. Details of tests in dry and wet conditions can be found in technical notes dating back to the 19th century. Although not every insulator was tested, in the 1940s all telephone insulators were tested - round about 5000 a week. This was a requirement of the Post Office. For the test, insulators were inverted in a large shallow trough and water run in. The interiors were then filled with water and the whole left to soak for twelve hours before being electrically tested by a girl for their insulating capacity. This process earned them the nickname of 'tumblers'. Apparently rejections were few.[21]

Porosity tests were also carried out for the Post Office by immersing broken insulators for 24 hours. When removed from the liquid there had to be no sign of impregnation. A sample of insulators was tested to destruction as a form of quality control. The insulators which were rejected were smashed and then they went to either a mill in Stanley or to another firm in Hanley called Harrisons, to be recycled back into the clay.

Courtesy of Taylor Tunnicliff Ltd

Milton Works c. 1925-30 showing ware exiting from Marlow tunnel oven No. 2.

Milton Works c. 1925-30 showing the fettling of die-pressed wares.

Courtesy of Taylor Tunnicliff Ltd

Hanley Works.
A section of the jolley shop
showing, in course of
production, a large carrier
wave insulator (background)
and a condenser bushing
weather shield (foreground)
c. 1925-30.

Courtesy of Taylor Tunnicliff Ltd

Albert Webb, fireman at Milton, c. 1940

J. Alcock

Milton Works c. 1950.
Staff of the Ovens department pictured inside an intermittent kiln with the
Ovens Manager Jack Benton standing in the centre.

Courtesy of Taylor Tunnicliff Ltd

Milton Works jolley shop c. 1925-30

Courtesy of Taylor Tunnicliff Ltd

Hanley Works spraying and dipping house c. 1925-30 showing immersion (left) and aerograph (right) processes.

Courtesy of Taylor Tunnicliff Ltd

Milton fettling shop showing ladies working on high tension pin-type insulators.

Courtesy of Taylor Tunnicliff Ltd

Milton Works c. 1925-30. Men packing insulators into saggars outside twenty-two chamber gas-fired oven battery

Milton Works c. 1925-30. Cementing metal fittings from Tipton into insulators and assembling multi-part insulators.

Courtesy of Taylor Tunnicliff Ltd

Courtesy of Taylor Tunnicliff Ltd

An unsuitable job for a woman? Milton testing laboratory c.1925-30. The photograph was captioned 'routine mechanical test', but had a hand-written instruction from management on the back to alter both figures to men.

Milton Works testing laboratory. The equipment on the right was used to pass an electrical current through the insulators c. 1940

Bullers' Insulators

Orders for insulators were noted in the company pattern books with detailed specifications. These original drawings are now in the possession of Stoke-on-Trent City Archives, safely preserved for posterity but, until the closure of the Milton works in 2001, were still used from time to time for the manufacture of replacement batches of insulators. New designs for insulators were prepared by company draughtsmen who prepared and drew detailed specifications, showing shrinkage calculations - usually 14%-15%. It was also necessary to create designs for accompanying fittings and processes as can be seen from the range of patents filed by the company. Wooden models of designs were sometimes made, both by Bullers or by the client company who sometimes sent a wooden sample with their order.

Unlike other branches of the pottery industry, insulators were not produced in standard sizes and sold from stock to customers. Each client had specific design requirements which had to be negotiated and accommodated, and so the making technology had to remain fairly basic and easy to adapt.

Costings were attached to the specification - costs being separately quoted for each operation in the making process - body; thrower; turner; biscuit firing; glost firing; cutting. For the die-pressed pieces the costings were based on body; making; drilling; biscuit firing; glost firing. Interestingly, there must have been some fear of industrial espionage and competition locally as many, perhaps more lucrative, ventures are costed in code. For Clark's patent insulator in 1875 costings in the pattern book resemble algebraic equations where letters, symbols and fractions are used rather than real numbers. Of course, Taylor Tunnicliff & Co. were also manufacturing similar products right next door so perhaps there was a suspicion that some information was being leaked from Bullers to their competitors.

This mutual suspicion is confirmed in the trade press as a quote from the Sentinel Yearbook of 1928 illustrates:

> "In the old days, when an electrical porcelain manufacturer had an inspiration and improved one of his processes, he, on principle, made it a "hush! hush!" matter, and his life was made miserable by the fear that his competitors would find out. Now he passes the information on and receives in return some hint which is just as valuable in another way."[22]

By 1877 Bullers were supplying insulators to the Post Office including the T129 which continued in use worldwide well into the 20th century. In co-operation with J.H. Cordeaux the specification for a screw thread inside an insulator was developed and in 1895 John Harris registered a patent for a new tool for cutting screw threads in hollow articles of clay.[23] The Cordeaux insulator became a worldwide standard because of its widespread use throughout the British Empire. Many orders from the period 1897-1898 specified the use of the Cordeaux screw, including one for His Highness the Nizam's Telephone Department (believed to be in Hyderabad, India).

The company not only produced their own designs for clients but also manufactured other patented designs under licence. In this context, order books mention Andrews, Varley, Heaviside, Clark and Johnson & Phillips amongst others. They also had a close working relationship with the London company W.T. Henley Telegraph Co. and manufactured many designs for them. They specialised in the manufacture of covered cables and their name was

Index to pattern books showing the T129 telephone insulator and its subsequent re-numbered variations.

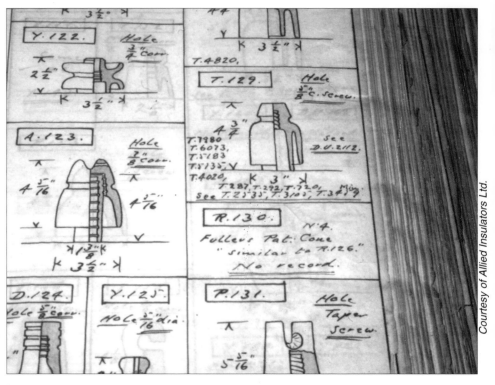

Courtesy of Allied Insulators Ltd.

synomynous with the development of telephone telegraphy.

The order books show the extent to which the company's products were in demand in this early period of telegraphic, transport and electric development. Railway companies and telephone companies were major clients. The former included:

* Caledonian Railway Co.
* Glasgow and South Western Railway
* Great Central Railway
* Great Eastern Railway
* Great North of Scotland Railway
* Great Western Railway Co.
* Lancashire & Yorkshire Railway
* North Staffordshire Railway
* South Devon Railway Co.

These insulators were sometimes marked with the initials of the purchasing company and are now sought after by collectors of railway memorabilia. Telephone companies worldwide used Bullers' insulators including:

* Yorkshire Telephone Co.
* National Telephone Co. (1892)
* United Telephone Co.
* Exchange Telephone Co. (1891)
* Telephone Co. of Ireland
* Mutual Telephone Co. (1892)
* Consolidated Telephone Construction Maintenance Co. Ltd. (1883)
* East Telephone Co.

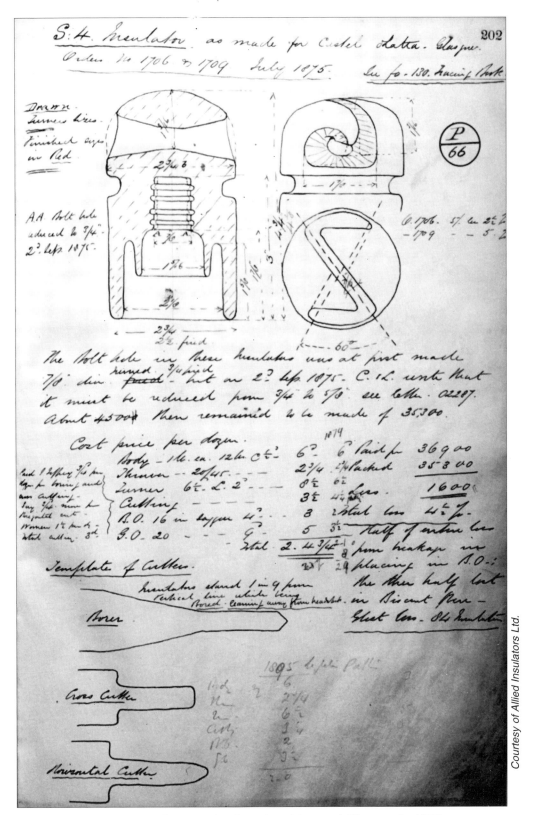

S4 insulator manufactured for Castel and Latta of Glasgow in 1875.
The drawing also shows the templates for the cutting and boring tools and the cost calculations

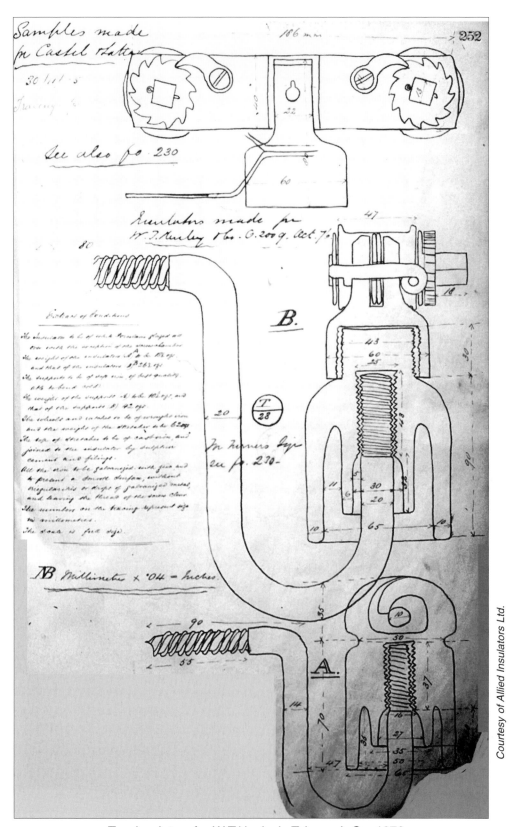

Two insulators for W.T.Henley's Telegraph Co, 1876.

* The Chili Tel. Co. (1893)
* Oriental Tel. Co. (1893)
* Tel. Co. of Egypt (1893)
* Natal Telephone Co. (1895)
* His Highness The Nizam's Telephone Dept. (1898)

In 1912, the British telephone system was taken over by the G.P.O. and they required Bullers to mark their insulators with these letters.[24] Other telephone components such as mouthpieces were also produced. (see p. 85)

Insulators were sent abroad by ship, one 1876 consignment going via Hull to Stavanger. The weight of the consignments gave cause for concern - on 26th November 1874 H.L. Schwab & Co. wrote that *"these insulators must be packed in smaller casks of 100 each."* The order book then notes that *"100 of these insulators can just be packed in a cask measuring 10 cub. Ft. Weight 2 cwt. 400 insulators = 1 shipping ton."*

A Glasgow company, Castel & Latta, ordered 35,000 insulators at 2s 4³/₄d per dozen in 1875. In 1876 they requested another design and the specification was written out in full to ensure that there were no misunderstandings: *"The Insulators must be of porcelain and of best quality & in one piece, perfectly enamelled both in the exterior surface, as also on the part destined to receive the screw of the support. With regard to the central cavity, it is necessary that the supports be screwed securely to the insulators by means of a light covering of rope yarn which the contractor will supply. When placed, the wire, reposing on the Insulator must be level with the centre of the screw fixed in the post. A deviation of 5 m/m only will be allowed."*

Instructions to the staff are often added in beside the technical drawing where there may have been past errors, such as *"Always ask 'What size spindle?'"* and, in 1890 on an order from London Electric Supply Corporation for an insulator made in two pieces: *"L.E.S. Cpn. afterwards said they wanted the Insulator to have been made in the ordinary way i.e. one piece. Quoted in Oct /90 for 100 at High figure as we do not want this work. E.M. (or E.W.)"*

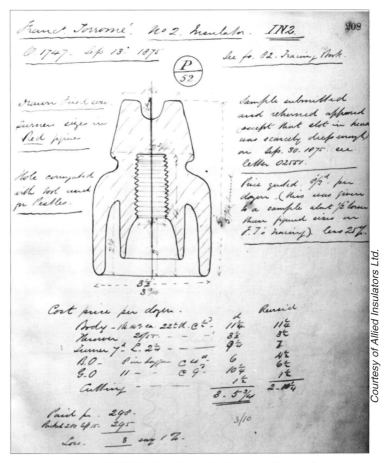

Drawing 1875 for insulator for Franco Torromé.

Courtesy of Allied Insulators Ltd.

Although renowned for high quality products, not all customers were satisfied. A blank page in the pattern book for pattern EA583 in 1891 states *"These were returned on a/c of inaccuracies so slight, that we let the work drop - the black ware was refused on a/c defective glaze"*. In those days the company were in a position to turn away difficult customers.

In 1885 the company expanded by merging with Jobson Brothers of Tipton who were engaged in similar work but had the additional benefit of an iron foundry thus providing an in-company source of metal attachments to accompany the insulators.[25] This company was known as Buller Jobson & Co. Ltd. and could now, from its two sites, provide the entire range of products needed for installation of new projects from within its own factories. A Buller Jobson & Co. catalogue of 1885 listed items for export to Canada, Spain, Australia, India, South America, Norway and Sweden, Italy, Portugal, and France.[26]

A salt-glazed insulator bearing the words PATENT BULLER, JOBSON & CO. LTD. DUDLEY suggests that perhaps the company were not only manufacturing insulators, but also buying in products (presumably specified by the customer) from other sources. There is no evidence to suggest that they themselves produced salt-glazed products, but Doultons did have a stoneware factory nearby at Dudley in the mid 19th century. Without being able to examine original order books for both companies this puzzle may remain unsolved. However, order books show that Jobson Brothers did order insulators from Bullers prior to the merger and so may have continued to buy in from other sources after the merger to satisfy specific customer requirements.

As high voltage generation and distribution spread worldwide, the company were well placed to supply this market. Large contracts included the Metropolitan Railway Third Rail electrification (1903); St. John Del Ray Mining Co. 11kV (using the first outdoor transmission line "pin" insulator made in two parts) (1904); Melbourne electrification (1910); Adelaide Tramways (1910); Newcastle-upon-Tyne 20kV system (1910); Victoria Falls 88kV (1911); Afghanistan 50kV (1911) and the Tata Hydro Electric Scheme 100kV (1911).

In the first half of the 20th century four major British projects kept the company order books full, quite apart from the large number of international contracts. They were the creation of the 132kV Transmission Grid (1930s); the 275kV Transmission Grid (1950s); 400kV Transmission Grid (1960s) and the electrification of British Railways.[27] During the First World War the company was "controlled" and was required to work night and day on government work, both military, naval and civilian. The company was placed in a similar position again during World War Two.

The world situation in 1914 gave the electrical porcelain manufacturers healthy profits. The trade press reported that Bullers' volume of business had exceeded any other year. They had realised a profit for the year of £18,058 and £1500 was to be spent on new machinery at Tipton. They acquired the Lichfield Pottery, previously owned by a Mr. Sandland, and MacIntyre (another insulator manufacturer) also had factory extensions underway.[28] By the end of 1914 Bullers' annual report showed a profit of £36,425 - double that of 1913.[29]

After the First World War, a consolidated annual report (1916-1919) was issued at the start of 1920. It illustrated how the company had benefitted financially from the hostilities. It stated that the directors had been unable to issue reports and statements of accounts during the War, being unable to arrive at accurate figures because of munitions levy and excess profits duty:

"The assessments have now been made and a settlement with the Government has been reached, enabling balance sheets for the four years to be submitted. The business of the company has been maintained with great success in spite of the abnormal difficulties presented by the war, and the directors congratulate the staff on their loyal and earnest prosecution of their strenuous duties. The conversion of the works from war to peace conditions has been most satisfactorily accomplished, and, in addition to the special depreciation allowed by the Government, a further amount of £5,000 has been hypothecated to meet the altered conditions of the Hanley works. In order to deal with the increase in the volume of business, new works at Milton are being erected, and are nearly complete, which will employ the most recent scientific methods and to manufacture material which has been hitherto largely imported from the Continent."[30]

The trade journal *Pottery Gazette and Glass Trades Review* provided some figures for the manufacture of electrical porcelain both in Staffordshire and overseas. In the 1926/27 period it noted that the German electrical porcelain industry had been stimulated by an increase in building contracts.[31] In 1927 it stated that seven English manufacturers (one of whom would have been Bullers) accounted for 95% of production of electrical porcelain[32] whilst the Sentinel Yearbook for 1928 noted that three extensive new electrical porcelain factories had recently been built.[33] Requests for companies to tender for work were placed in the British trade press by overseas companies such as Ritsema & Co., Hilversum, Holland who placed this advertisement in 1920: *"We are seeking Porcelain Factory which is open to make continuous large quantities of patented PORCELAIN FITTINGS FOR ELECTRICAL PURPOSES. The fitting is very simple and of small size. Million pieces can be ordered."* [34] Bullers would almost certainly have tendered for this.

A 1930 newspaper article was confident of Bullers' continued success as market leader. It stated: *"It is the achievements of their products which have established the unique position of Bullers, Ltd. There need be no fear of the company's position not continuing to be recognised as that of leader in the British electro-technical porcelain industry. That this will be the case is the confident belief of the whole organisation (numbering some 2000), from the youngest "hand" to senior member of the Board of Directors, each of whom is British and zealous in maintaining the British tradition of the company and its founder."*[35]

After the War there was a demand for 2,500 more workers to make insulators and fittings to meet the National Housing Plan.[36] In this report the trade unions complained that the electrical porcelain industry was drawing people away from the china and earthenware works. Ex-staff have commented that Bullers was not known for good wages, but perhaps secure employment in a growth industry was sufficient to attract workers. The demand for insulators ensured the company remained in a healthy financial state during this period and supported some diversification into other areas.

The company did not only produce large insulators - many small low tension insulating components were manufactured, such as for spark plugs (for Keeling and Walker), for cookers, light fittings and electric fires. The sizes ranged from some so small that many could be fitted into a matchbox up to insulators 17 feet high and weighing 2 tons. By 1967 the company was the largest manufacturer of electrical porcelain in Europe.[37] The installation of a new Axiturn automated vertical lathe, the operation of which was controlled by punched paper tape, cut the forming time for a 7 foot 6 inch insulator from forty minutes to sixteen.

Following the move of Taylor Tunnicliff to Milton in 1981 some technical changes had to be made to the methods of production. Taylor Tunnicliff fired at a lower temperature than Bullers (1180-1190 degrees, compared to Bullers 1230-1240 degrees), thus saving fuel costs. When their Stone factory closed and all production was moved to Milton both the clay body and the glazes had to be altered to accommodate both companies' methods. On some designs in the insulator pattern books changes have been noted as being for the "T.T. body".

Bullers were the first electrical porcelain manufacturers in Staffordshire to change over from "town gas" to liquid petroleum gas, in the form of butane and this took place in 1969. This was said by the technical press to demonstrate *an optimism which is a reflection of the company's faith in its product*.[38]

The quantity and variety of insulating products produced by Bullers was staggering. In this book it is only possible to highlight some historical details of these productions rather than the technical details. In 1905 a press reporter visiting the factory said:

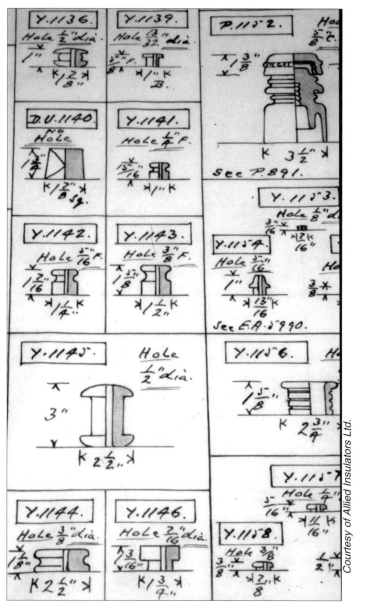

Small insulators shown in the index to the pattern books.

Courtesy of Allied Insulators Ltd.

"A merely casual inspection of the warehouses, and, indeed, of the works generally, leads the visitor to the conclusion that the whole habitable globe lives and moves and has its being wholly and solely for the sake of insulators of one size or shape or another. There are everywhere piles, stacks, racks or mountains of insulators. Right and left, upstairs and downstairs, everywhere in fact, one sees insulators, breathes insulators, talks insulators - and, indeed, one is perfectly certain after some hours of inspection that insulators are the only mundane objects which merit the slightest attention at the hands of an electrified humanity."[39]

This author may have been quite correct!

REFERENCES

1. Infringement of a patent. Ford v. Buller in *Staffordshire Advertiser* 27th June 1851 p.3
2. Scarratt, William. *Old Times in the Potteries*. Scarratt, 1906
3. Notices in *Staffordshire Advertiser* 23rd June 1849 p.1 col.1 and 8th February 1851 p.1 col.2
4. Ford, Charles. UK patent no. 11488 Improvements in the manufacture of pottery or earthenware and in the tools, instruments, or apparatus employed therein, part or parts of which improvements are applicable to other similar purposes. 1846
5. Infringement of a patent. Op. cit.
6. Ford, Charles. UK patent no. 11488. Manufacture of pottery. Ford's disclaimer and memorandum of alteration. 1851.
7. Buller, Thomas Wentworth. UK patent no. 12599. Improvements in the manufacture of earthenware. 1849
8. Buller, Wentworth and Mugford, Jabez Hearn. UK patent no. 3194. Improvements in spur-supporting rings for fixing plates, dishes and other like articles in glost ovens. 1862
9. Pennell, Isaac and Harris, John Thomas. UK patent no. 10817. Improved apparatus or appliance for use in supporting ceramic-ware in enamel-kilns whilst being fired. 1891.
10. Buller, Ernest Wentworth. UK patent no. 1232. Improvements in attaching door and other knobs may be applied to the manufacture of the terminal ornaments of metallic furniture and other articles. 1870.
11. Bullers advertisement in *Ceramics* August 1967
12. Taylor Tunnicliff Ltd. Bullers Rings. Promotional leaflet. c.2001
13. Staffordshire Sentinel Ltd. *The Sentinel Yearbook* 1928. p.37
14. Watkin, Ernest. Address to the Ceramic Society in *Pottery Gazette and Glass Trade Review* 1st May 1924. p.835
15. Wade, Major G.A. Manufacture of electrical porcelain in *Cox's Pottery Annual and Glass Trade Year Book*. 1926. p.85
16. The manufacture of insulators in *Electrical Power* March 1905 p.49-53
17. Johnson, P. and Robinson, W.G. Development of pottery bodies - electrical porcelain. Paper delivered at a meeting of the Pottery Section, Trentham Gardens, Stoke-on-Trent, 22nd October 1974
18. Child J. The Staffordshitre Potteries as an Empire Asset; Souvenir of the Royal Visit. Manchester 1913
19. Wade, Major G.A. Manufacture of electrical porcelain in *Pottery Gazette Annual and Glass Trades Yearbook* 1926 p.87
20. Brent, W.H. *Porcelain Insulators*. The Post Office Green Papers no.10. 1934
21. Brent. Op. cit.
22. Staffordshire Sentinel Ltd. *Sentinel Year Book of the Potteries and North Staffordshire*. 1928. p.37
23. Harris, John Thomas. UK patent no. 13387. A new or improved tool or appliance for cutting screw threads in hollow articles of clay or other soft materials. 1895
24. Albers, M. and Tod, J. *Worldwide Porcelain Insulators*. p.14
25. Agreement [merger of Bullers Ltd and Jobson Brothers] 20th May 1885
26. Albers, M. and Tod, J. Op. cit.
27. Bullers Limited. Unpublished company history.
28. *Pottery Gazette and Glass Trades Review* 1st January 1914
29. *Pottery Gazette and Glass Trades Review* 1st December 1914
30. Bullers Ltd in *Pottery Gazette and Glass Trade Review* 2nd February 1920. p.247
31. *Pottery Gazette and Glass Trade Review* 1st September 1926 and 1st October 1927
32. *Pottery Gazette and Glass Trade Review* 1st December 1927
33. *Sentinel Yearbook* 1928. Op. cit.
34. Miscellaneous advertisements in *Pottery Gazette and Glass Trade Review* 1st July 1920. p.840
35. British electro-technical pottery in *Financial Times* 16th July 1930
36. Notes and news in *Pottery and Glass* June 1946 p.42
37. High voltage porcelain insulators in *Ceramics* June 1967. p.45
38. Fernie, K. & Price, E.E. Bullers change to butane in *Ceramics* November 1969 p.14-22
39. The manufacture of insulators. Op. cit.

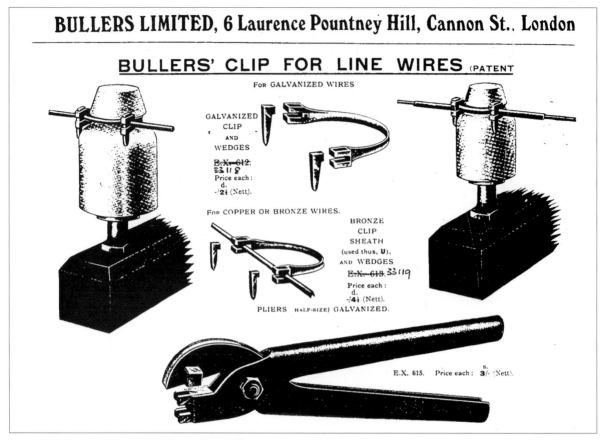

From an early catalogue.

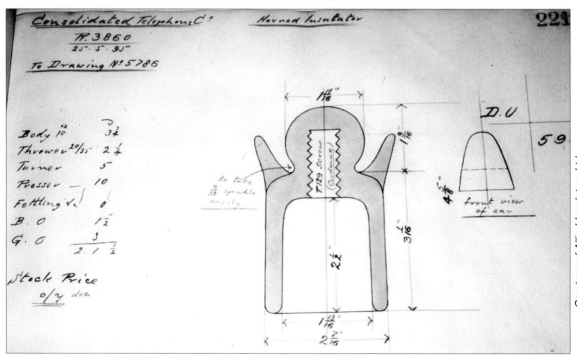

Horned insulator for The Consolidated Telephone Co. 1895.

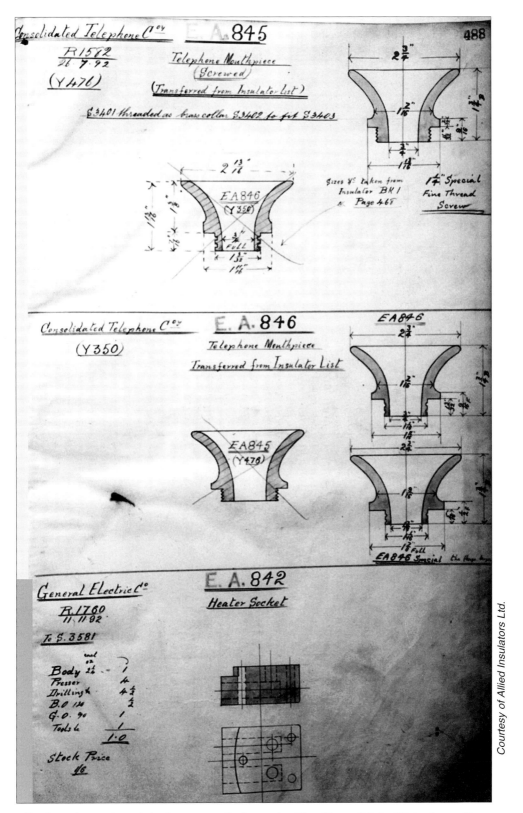

Designs for various telephone mouthpieces for The Consolidated Telephone Co. and a heater socket for the General Electric Co. 1892.

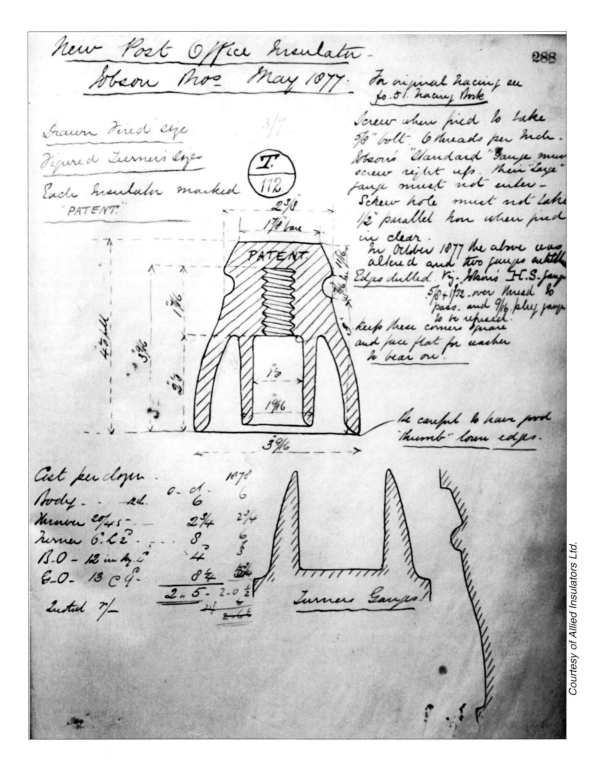

Drawing for new Post Office insulator T112 for Jobson Bros of Dudley, 1877.

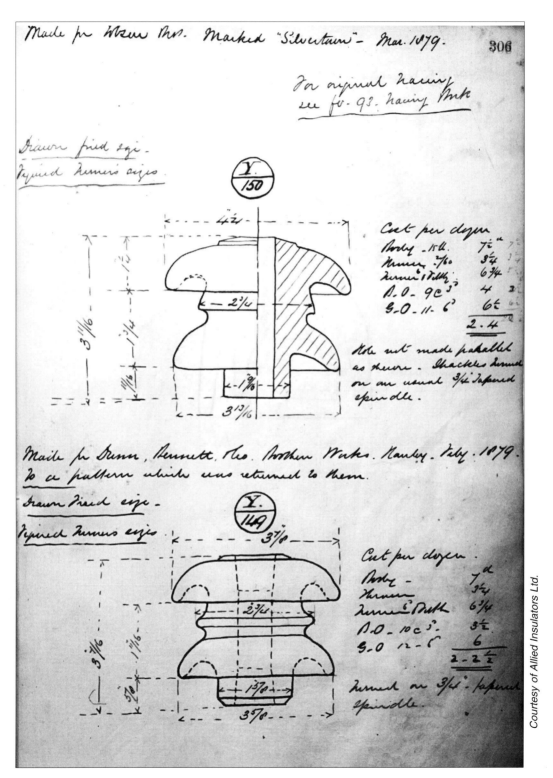

Two insulator designs 1879.
The top one is for Jobson Bros, Dudley, the company with whom Bullers later merged.
The bottom insulator was for Dunn, Bennett & Co of Hanley.

Courtesy of Allied Insulators Ltd.

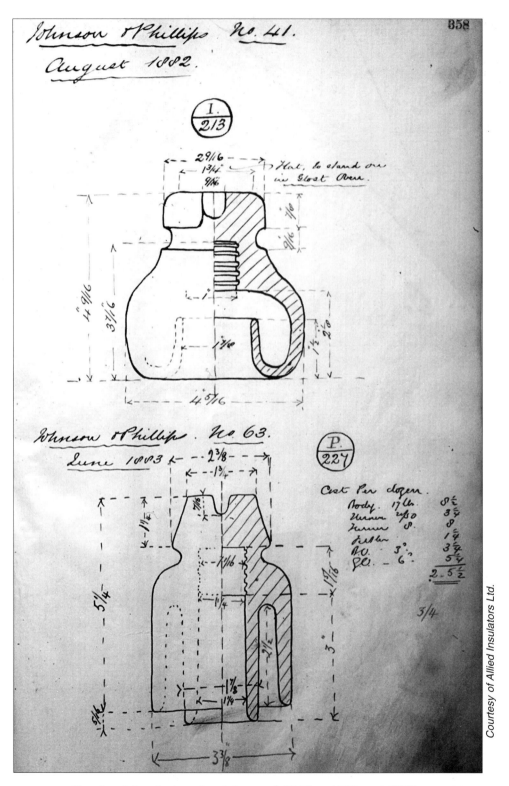

Two insulator designs for Johnson & Phillips 1882 and 1883.

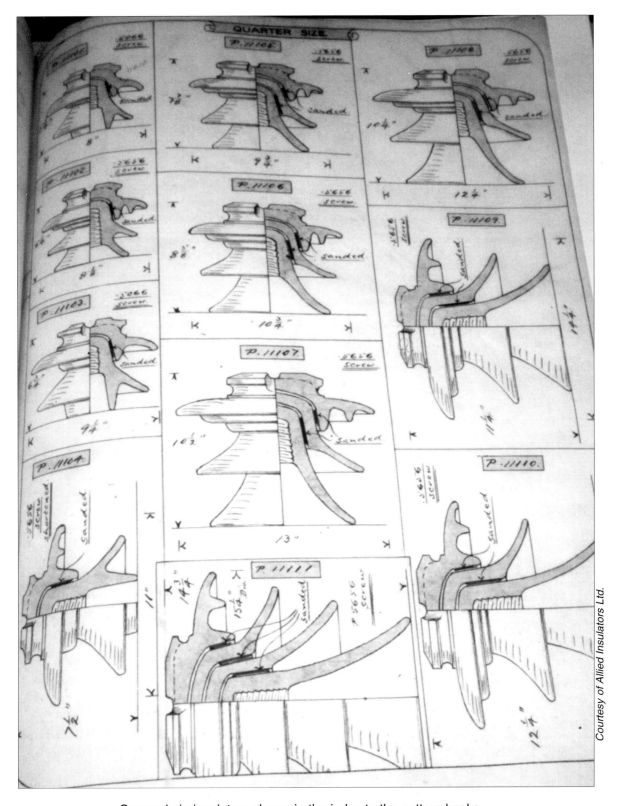

Cap and pin insulators shown in the index to the pattern books.

Courtesy of Allied Insulators Ltd.

Milton Works packing and despatch shed c 1925-30. Crates were made here and insulators packed in straw.

Courtesy of Taylor Tunnicliff Ltd

The pressing shop at Milton c. 1925-30

Courtesy of Taylor Tunnicliff Ltd

High Tension Insulators.

Particulars of Tests.

Insulator	Sketch	Dry Test. Discharge takes place over surface at :—	Under Spray. Flash passes over surface at :—	Dripping wet but without spray. Flash passes over surface at :—
S. 18743 Dg 20661 P. 2963 27.2.08		Tests to :— 60.000 Volts. (without sheath)	50,000 Volts.	Tests to 60.000 Volts without sparking.
Dg. 19559 27.2.08		Tests to 60.000 Volts.	40.000 Volts.	Tests to 60.000 Volts.
Dg. 19419 27.2.08		Tests to 60.000 Volts.	40.000 Volts.	Tests to 60.000 Volts, but with considerable noise.
Dg. 19958 27.2.08 P. 2399		Tests to 60.000 Volts.	50.000 Volts.	Tests to 60.000 Volts.
Dg. 18919 27.2.08 P. 2324		Tests to 60.000 Volts.	42.000 Volts.	Flash passes at 60.000 Volts.
Dg. 21344 27.2.08 P. 1897		Discharge takes place at 55.000 Volts.	30,000 Volts.	Flash passes at 35.000 Volts.
Dg. 19312 27.2.08 P. 1628		Tests perfectly to 60,000 Volts.	35.000 Volts.	Flash passes at 60.000 Volts.
Dg. 14839 27.2.08		Tests perfectly to 60.000 Volts.	50.000 Volts.	Tests to 60.000 Volts.
P. 3135 31.8.10		withstood 55,000 Volts.	withstood 20,000 Volts. Flashed over at 30,000 Spray = 2" Rain in 5 Minutes	

Details of tests for high tension insulators under wet and dry conditions.

BULLERS LIMITED, 6 Laurence Pountney Hill, Cannon St., London.

E.P. CLASS.   INSULATORS FITTED.

Scale about ⅓rd full size. All Insulators supplied in White Porcelain unless other color asked for.

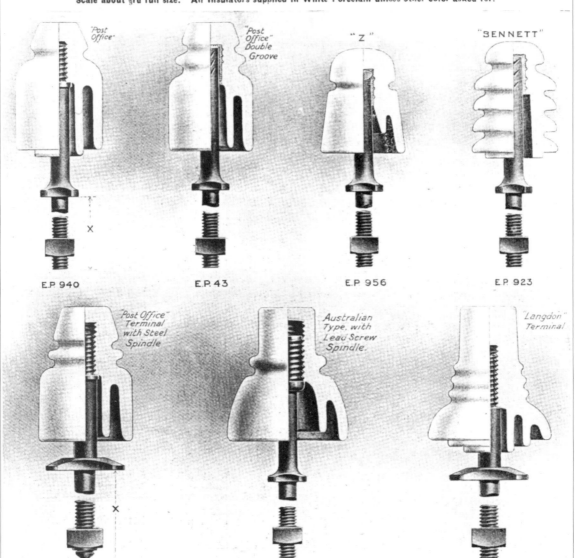

Catalogue Number.	Size of Insulator.				Approx. weight of one Insulator.		Dimensions of Spindle at "X."		Approx. weight of one Spindle.		Price per doz.
	Diameter.		Height.								
	in.	m/m	in.	m/m	lbs.	Kgms.	in. in.	m/m m m	lbs.	Kgms	s. d.
E.P. 940	3 1/16	(78)	4¾	(121)	1·53	(·695)	3⅝ × ⅝	(92 × 15·9)	1·05	(·476)	8/9
E.P. 43	2⅞	(73)	4 9/16	(116)	1·22	(·553)	3⅝ × ⅝	(92 × 15·9)	·97	(·440)	9/9
E.P. 956	3 1/16	(78)	3⅝	(92)	·94	(·427)	3⅝ × ⅝	(92 × 15·9)	·70	(·318)	8/3
E.P. 923	3⅛	(79)	4⅛	(105)	1·53	(·695)	3⅝ × ⅝	(92 × 15·9)	·78	(·354)	10/6
E.P. 227	3 15/32	(88)	4¾	(121)	1·83	(·831)	4⅛ × ¾	(105 × 19)	2·04	(·925)	14/3
E.P. 239	4¼	(108)	4¾	(121)	1·91	(·867)	3⅝ × ⅝	(92 × 15·9)	1·65	(·749)	13/-
E.P. 240	4 7/16	(113)	5 3/16	(132)	2·17	(·984)	4¼ × ¾	(108 × 19)	1·73	(·785)	15/3

D Mycock

Albert Bailey in Milton sticking-up shop.

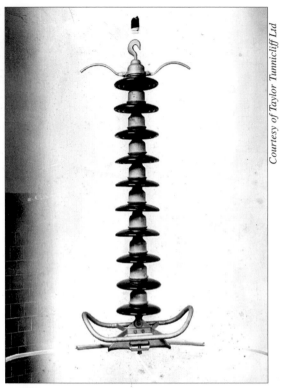

Courtesy of Taylor Tunnicliff Ltd

'Flashover' test on a string insulator c.1930

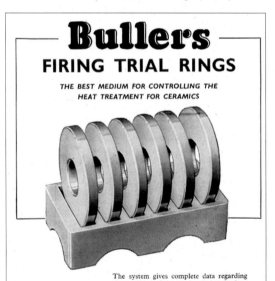

Bullers
FIRING TRIAL RINGS

*THE BEST MEDIUM FOR CONTROLLING THE
HEAT TREATMENT FOR CERAMICS*

**REGULARLY USED BY
MORE THAN 300 POTTERY
& BRICK MANUFACTURERS**

The rings at the present time being used in the manufacture of Grinding Wheels, Bricks, Refractories, Electrical Porcelain, China, Earthenware, Sanitary Ware, Tiles, etc.

The system gives complete data regarding the condition of the product being fired, at all times and from all sections of the kiln. It also enables the Management to keep in touch with the firing of the kiln and to know exactly how it is proceeding.

Various racks have been designed to meet the demand for a convenient means of setting the rings on Tunnel Trucks and in Intermittent Kilns, in fact for all conditions where easy withdrawal of the rings during firing is desired.

BULLERS LIMITED

JOINERS SQUARE WORKS · HANLEY · STOKE-ON-TRENT
Telephone : Stoke-on-Trent 22341   Telegrams : Bullers, Hanley

1967 trade advertisement.

SOME of the largest and most intricate pieces of Electro Technical Pottery ever produced have been manufactured by Bullers and their Modern Potteries at Hanley and Milton are capable of dealing with any specification for Electrical Porcelain.

A staff of Designers and Electrical Engineers is maintained whose experience and service is at your disposal on all problems of Insulation.

Enquiries are invited for any type of Electrical Porcelain Insulation.

Bullers Limited

6, LAURENCE POUNTNEY HILL, LONDON, E.C. 4.
Tel : City 985 & 986.   Telegrams : "Bullers, Cannon, London."
PORCELAIN WORKS: HANLEY & MILTON, STAFFS.
IRON WORKS: TIPTON, STAFFS.

1925 trade advertisement

Chapter 3

THE FORMATION OF THE BULLERS' ART POTTERY STUDIO

Gordon Forsyth

In the late 1920s a series of fortuitous coincidences led to the creation of what has come to be recognised as an art pottery studio within the Bullers' works at Milton. In 1920 Stoke-on-Trent had appointed, as their new Superintendent of Art Education, a forward-looking and outspoken individual, Gordon Forsyth.[1] He saw his role as not simply to co-ordinate the work of the art schools in the various towns of the Potteries, but to strive for improvements in the design of pottery by working closely with the manufacturers, thus making the work of the art schools more relevant to the needs of the local industries. His particular interest was in the pottery industry but, of course, the art schools did prepare students for work in other industries such as signwriting, printing, millinery and leather work. One of his other official roles was as Art Adviser to the British Pottery Manufacturers' Federation.[2]

Forsyth's own background was initially that of a trained painter but he had diversified into other aspects of the decorative arts such as stained glass and, before coming to the Potteries, had been the Art Director at Pilkington's Tile and Pottery Company in Clifton near Manchester. This company had originally been established in 1891 to manufacture bricks from local clays but abandoned this product in favour of tiles, which had become popular decorative items during the Victorian period. It was a new factory and opened in 1893. In 1903 the company manager William Burton decided the company should expand into decorative glazed pottery and set up a small art pottery department producing a range of goods known as "Lancastrian Pottery".[3]

When Forsyth arrived at Pilkington's as Art Director in 1905 he was only 25 years old. He found a small group of skilled ceramic artists working in a studio environment with dedicated throwers and technical experts from the industrial setting. His role was to further develop the range of studio wares upon which Burton's glazes could be best displayed. He himself produced many elaborate designs at Pilkington's, often in lustres and featuring detailed calligraphy and heraldic devices. Forsyth and Burton gained a reputation for encouraging free expression amongst the throwers and artists of the studio, allowing their personalities to be displayed in their work. The company sponsored some of their employees to attend art school classes.[4]

Forsyth undertook many commissioned pieces at Pilkington's, both tile panels and decorated

Gordon M Forsyth. Photograph given to his secretary, Hilda Thomas, sister of thrower Harold Thomas, in November 1944.

vessels. Some of these were for clients in Stoke-on-Trent so his skills were already known in the area. Whilst working in the Potteries he continued to produce work for local commissions and these included stained glass windows for local churches such as St. Joseph's Church, Burslem and Sacred Heart Church, Tunstall[5] and illuminated manuscripts for the town council and other organisations. A letter from the Prime Minister, Stanley Baldwin, written in his own hand to Gordon Forsyth in 1928 attests to the quality of his work:

"Dear Mr Forsyth, I have never had an Address presented to me so completely satisfactory in style, colour and design as the one given to me the other day at Stoke. ......I am therefore emboldened to tell you what keen pleasure it has given me and how I rejoice that you are in Stoke to draw out and train that talent that is indigenous to our soil."[6]

Whilst at Pilkington's he began to teach part-time at Manchester Art School and was also a visiting lecturer at Glasgow School of Art. This experience plus his industrial experience made him an ideal candidate for the post in charge of the Stoke-on-Trent art schools.

Forsyth restructured the art schools of the Potteries towns making Burslem School of Art the main centre for art education and basing himself there. He put in place a scholarship system which encouraged talented pupils from less well off backgrounds to attend art school classes part-time. In 1925 he established a Junior Art Department at Burslem which was to offer a full educational curriculum for its students but with a strong emphasis on the arts as its main thrust.[7] This course proved to be the training ground of many talented artists and designers, some of whom moved on to work in the studio at Bullers' Milton factory.

Forsyth was a regular speaker and participant at the various society and industry meetings in the area. By building up contacts at managerial and art director level within the industry he established links between the work of the art schools and industrial processes. Not only was he highly influential and controversial within the Potteries, but his reputation was also known nationally and he was in touch with most of the leading proponents of modern industrial design in London. From 1920 - 1924 he was a Fellow of the British Society of Industrial Art.[8]

Forsyth put in place arrangements with some local pottery companies to supply the art schools with blank wares for the students to decorate. These included standard shapes such as dinner plates, vegetable serving dishes and even cube teapot sets. One such company whose sponsorship he cultivated was Bullers. It seems likely that he approached Bullers via Guy Harris as they both attended local meetings of the Ceramic Society and they shared a common interest in Chinese porcelains and their glazes. They are reported

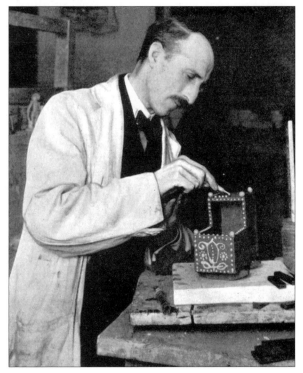

Gordon M Forsyth in Burslem School of Art slip decorating an earthenware cradle.

William Ruscoe and his students at Burslem School of Art c. 1932

William Ruscoe and his students at Burslem School of Art c. 1932. The student on the right is making a roll figure.

as having technical discussions with other potters such as Charles Noke of Doultons who gathered at evening meetings in Forsyth's Burslem School of Art.[9]

The limited facilities at local art schools only permitted firing of earthenware and not high temperature clay bodies such as stoneware and porcelain and so some assistance from the industry was required if students were to gain experience of working with these materials. One of Forsyth's staff, William Ruscoe (of whom more later) remembered Guy Harris as being instrumental in getting a high temperature gas-fired kiln installed in the Burslem School of Art and that he instructed Ruscoe in the operation of this machine. In order to obtain the best results from this new kiln, Bullers supplied what was described by Ruscoe as generous amounts of clay body and glazes for the students to work with. [10]

Gordon Forsyth harboured ambitions to advance the art school - industry connection further than this and suggested that the schools could act as experimental units for industrial prototypes.[11] He knew that there were precedents for art pottery studios existing within industrial ceramic enterprises. The best known within the field of British ceramics was probably the Doulton Lambeth studio of the late 19th century which operated within their saltglazed stoneware drainpipe factory. In Stoke-on-Trent in the first half of the 20th century there were also examples of art pottery wares being produced within both tile and sanitary ware manufacturers such as Richards Tiles and Howsons.

Forsyth also looked to the continent for inspiration and had studied the organisation and methods of the Bauhaus school in Germany, referring to them in 1921 as an interesting school of designers who made use of art in a commercial sense.[12] The studios of the Scandinavian manufacturers such as Orrefors (Sweden) and Arabia (Finland) also provided new models for designers working and experimenting within industrial concerns.

One of the aspirations of the Bauhaus was that it should produce design prototypes which could then be adopted by industry for mass production. At the Bauhaus an active pottery production unit existed based away from the main school in a village where a country pottery tradition already existed. The students there were expected to produce work for sale to raise income for the school.[13] It seems likely that Forsyth was looking for an opportunity to create a model of this type in Stoke-on-Trent as an example for other companies to follow.

Although his commitments as Superintendent of Art Education restricted his own output of work, Forsyth did himself produce some pieces at Bullers in conjunction with the artists and potters based there. With Forsyth as its inspiration we can divide the work of Bullers' Studio into two distinct periods - the early period which consisted mainly of the work of Anne Potts, Guy Harris and Gordon Forsyth and the later, longer period under the direction of Agnete Hoy.

Anne Potts

In 1934 the Burslem School of Art - Bullers connection was finally cemented with the creation of a studio on the Bullers' premises at Milton. This was to be run by Anne Potts, one of the students from the Burslem School of Art Junior Art Department whom Forsyth recommended to the Harris management team for the position.

In 1933 she had been one of several pupils from Burslem whose work was shown at the *Exhibition of British Industrial Art in Relation to the Home* at

Porcelain bowl with crackle glaze by Gordon Forsyth c. 1940. The calligraphic inscription is typical of his work.

Dorland Hall, London. The Burslem exhibit consisted of 57 figures described as *'Glazed pottery in red and cane clays decorated with coloured slips'*, three of which were by Potts. They were no.

577 'Beg' at 5 shillings; no. 581 'Gossips' at 7 shillings and sixpence (now in the Potteries Museum & Art Gallery, Stoke-on-Trent); and no. 589 'The Thriller' at 7 shillings and sixpence. William Ruscoe and Frank Scott, teachers at Burslem, also exhibited work there in the same style as their students.[14] Ruscoe recalled in his autobiography the unexpected success of the student pieces in this national exhibition, telling how they sold out. This prompted the stamping of future figures with a Staffordshire knot and the initials B.S.A. for Burslem School of Art. When several retailers asked the school to produce more such figures, it was decided that, as it was inappropriate for the school to become a production centre, the figures should be made in outside workshops. Ruscoe's own workshop became such a studio, employing some of the students and so Gordon Forsyth now had some hard evidence of possible commercial demand to show to Bullers.[15]

At the time of her appointment to the staff at Bullers, Anne Potts was only 16 years of age. Although today this seems a rather early age to have been placed in such a responsible position we must remember that in both the pottery industry and at home it was then quite usual for young girls to be left in charge and for people to start work from as young as 14 years old. Members of her family have said that she was used to assuming a position of responsibility within the family home and so would not have found her new work situation too daunting. She continued to study at Burslem part-time (a common practice in the pottery industry) and at Bullers she worked closely with Guy Harris who created the glazes for the studio productions.

Harris and Potts were assisted by a thrower from the factory, Fred Weir. His previous work had been throwing porcelain insulators which were much thicker and heavier than decorative wares and some early pieces were therefore very heavy, illustrating the difficulty found in working with this type of clay. A fellow student from Burslem, Joyce Cooper, also came to the studio in 1939 as an assistant modeller. She later became an assistant to John Wadsworth at Mintons.[16]

During this early period another potter named John Cottrell worked in the studio for about a year. He was already known as a studio potter and had been a student of William Staite Murray at the Royal College of Art prior to coming to Bullers. He had exhibited at the Brygos Gallery, London in 1936 and Bullers donated some of his smaller pieces to a 1938 exhibition of stoneware held at Hanley Museum.[17] Being

A & J Marshall

Anne Potts (left) outside the Milton Works, with her assistant Joyce Cooper

A & J Marshall

Noah's Ark by Anne Potts.
Modelled in porcelain at Bullers.

A & J Marshall

A & J Marshall

Two figure groups produced by
Anne Potts at Bullers.

of a stoneware body his wares are markedly different in style from Anne Potts' work, and were thrown and glazed in mainly dark colours. It is not clear what brought Cottrell to Bullers or why he chose to work in stoneware rather than porcelain.

Many of the early pieces of work produced by Anne Potts were modelled figures and small decorative pieces which reflected the teachings of the aforementioned Burslem School of Art modelling master William Ruscoe. Ruscoe taught the making of roll figures, a type of ware which he himself produced in quantity. The figures were originally intended as a task which the students could complete in the three quarters of an hour allocated to the modelling class.[18] The subject matter of the Burslem figure groups are scenes and animals from the daily lives of the students with titles such as 'Carpenter', 'Dennis the Dachshund' and 'Market Day'.

The Potteries Museum & Art Gallery

William Ruscoe holding one of his figure groups

Potts' early roll figure groups display a student naivety which is perhaps emphasised by the coarse earthenware body commonly in use at Burslem. In contrast, the pieces produced in Bullers' porcelain reflect her development as an artist with fine detail and composition. Freed from the restrictions of the classroom situation, she was able to design more complex and time-consuming pieces.

For the subject matter of her figures, Potts mainly used acquaintances and scenes from the factory and also from the Potteries towns. A self portrait exists and also one of her colleague in the studio, Joyce Cooper. Both figures are shown working at their benches with cups, handles, decorating tools and pottery figures. Her mentor, Gordon Forsyth, was featured in a model of an art student and teacher, and the factory saggar maker with the foreman, Will Huyton, also formed a group. Figures of hikers, card players, lovers on a bench, Christopher Robin, and women gossiping, are also known to exist.

A large and complex piece known as 'Company Car' depicted Gilbert Harris looking anxiously out of the company car window as the chauffeur Robert Pierpoint lay underneath trying to fix a problem. The firing of such pieces must have required a considerable amount of support for all the component parts, and some distortion can be seen in this particular model. Many of these portrait pieces inevitably went straight into

D Jeffery

the ownership of either the people depicted or Bullers' management and remain in private hands today.

Anne Potts was particularly deft at producing very small scale but perfectly formed models of animals. Members of the Harris family recall being taken to the studio by their father where she would quickly produce small animals for their amusement and encourage them to make their own models with the clay. These would later be fired and sent home for them. Many of these animals and plant forms are only an inch or so high and so whilst creating them for the children she was perhaps also using these as experiments or prototypes for larger and more ambitious compositions.

Examples of these more complex modelled pieces included Noah's Arks, with the miniature animals grouped together on a base. Five Noah's arks are said to have been made but only one is still known to survive.[19] Potts' assistant Joyce Cooper also made many of the small animal figures used in the compositions. Work of a more practical and perhaps more commercial nature included bookends, where the modelled figures or animals rested against a slab of clay which formed the end piece.

In 1935 a further exhibition entitled *British Art in Industry* was held in London and to this Bullers contributed 58 pieces, [see Appendix 4] participating alongside many of the 'big names' of the Potteries such as Wedgwood (showing wares designed for them by Keith Murray), and Wood and Sons (showing Susie Cooper designs on their pottery). Gordon Forsyth's involvement in these large nationally publicised exhibitions ensured Bullers' participation whilst some other larger companies seemingly chose to ignore such events. At an address to the Royal Society of Arts in 1934 (a body far removed from industrial manufacture) he highlighted the work of the Bullers' studio, saying *"Very little hard paste porcelain has been manufactured by British potters in recent years, with the exception of the excellent porcelain made by the electrical equipment manufacturers. It is therefore a matter of real interest to find at least one firm of porcelain manufacturers turning their attention to the production of decorative pottery in this splendid material."*[20]

The 1935 catalogue listed a wide range of ornamental wares (vases, dishes, plaques etc.) with an astonishing range of glazes. The fifteen pieces specifically credited to Potts are mostly models of people and animals. The prices for these works ranged from five shillings to ten shillings and sixpence. We do not know how many of these pieces were sold.[21]

Unfortunately there are no known photographs of the Bullers pieces at the 1935 exhibition. A flambé vase was on offer at a price of £2. 2/-, the most expensive piece. This does seem to confirm that Bullers were still treating the studio as an experimental venture rather than as a serious commercial venture. They may have considered that gaining exposure for their technical and artistic success in this London arena was reward enough for their ceramics which were certainly never intended to be the main products of the factory. Certainly, for the young Anne Potts it must have been an exciting time.

Although Potts is best remembered for her figure work it would be wrong to suggest that this was her sole contribution to the studio output. A few rare examples exist of vases attributed to Potts but unfortunately these are not always marked or signed to assist in identification (most of her figures do bear a signature). One fine vase decorated in sgraffito work shows the influence of oriental wares, the incised decoration in black slip showing the white porcelain body below. Another piece is decorated in relief with modelled figures and animals of a similar style to the roll-modelled figures. Some other pieces were 'commissioned' for the Harris family as gifts to friends and family, and bear the initials of the intended recipient and sometimes the year of production.

Other, more practical, tablewares were also made in the studio around this period. Jugs and mugs of a plain barrel shape were cast and produced in sets. Although plain and, to an extent, modernist in shape, they were often decorated with unusual brightly coloured and lustrous glazes created by Guy Harris. Similar wares had been produced by Keith Murray at Wedgwood and several designers of the period sought to emulate his shapes. Such was the practicality of the design that Bullers continued to produce these mugs for several years. They apparently cost £2. 8s 0d per dozen when first made.[22] Together with the jug they would have been sold as cider or beer sets. The larger jugs are very heavy, reflecting the thick potting required to master the porcelain.

In 1939 Anne Potts married and left the Bullers studio. With the onset of war Bullers understandably did not actively seek to keep the studio open, their production of the more essential electrical porcelain goods being both a company and government priority.

Anne Potts moved south and continued her work as a studio potter later producing animals, figure groups and jewellery. Unfortunately she suffered from arthritis in later life which curtailed her pottery career.

Guy Harris

The studio could not have produced such a range of innovative wares without the skills of Bullers' glaze chemist Guy Harris. It is unclear how he developed his skills as a glaze chemist. A background in agricultural engineering and a love of nature and the countryside would not

seem the most obvious qualifications for the position which he held in Bullers but his talents were undoubted and all who worked with him spoke highly of his abilities. His position in management allowed him the time to devote to this work which was primarily a hobby, albeit a technically challenging one. Other members of the Harris family do not seem to have taken the same active interest in the studio, although John Waugh, John Elvine and Gilbert Harris did visit the studio, and supported its continuation.

His work on the decorative wares allowed him the opportunity to experiment in the re-creation of a wide range of Chinese-inspired glazes. Staff who worked with him remember a cupboard in his laboratory which contained shelves of tiny insulators demonstrating the range of decorative glazes and effects which he had achieved. The results of the trials were all recorded and the insulators numbered. He was a frequent visitor to Hanley Museum and actively supported their work,

Guy Harris, President of the British Ceramic Society 1947-48

donating pieces to and opening an exhibition of stoneware in 1938.[23] The museum curator, Geoffrey Bemrose, and he were both involved in the North Staffordshire Field Club and their friendship allowed him access to the museum collections for study purposes. Some pieces were cast from designs of items in that collection but it is not known who created the moulds for these.[24] Guy Harris had sustained a permanent injury to his arm prior to his work with Bullers and this prevented him from being able to throw pottery himself. He could have made the moulds or could have called on the expertise of factory staff for this work.

EXHIBITION AT MUSEUM

Mr. Guy Harris, who opened the exhibition of ancient and modern stoneware pottery at the Hanley Museum, with Mr. H. Booth (who presided) and Mr. G. J. V. Bemrose (Curator).

Extract from *The Sentinel* 1938.

An example of one of Guy Harris's crackle glazes was recently featured on a Royal Mail Millennium postage stamp, in the series 'Art and Craft'. This stamp was a close-up of the surface of a dish with a pink and grey crackle effect glaze from the Potteries Museum & Art Gallery collection. It was chosen to represent the Stoke-on-Trent Millennium project Ceramica, in Burslem, but unfortunately neither Bullers nor Guy Harris were named on the stamp.

The work of the studio ceased temporarily after the departure of Anne Potts in 1939. Pieces produced during this early period are not always marked. Anne Potts normally marked her pieces by incising into the base *"Anne Potts Made in England by Bullers"*. On other items, such as vases and mugs, a printed stamp was used with the words *BULLERS MADE IN ENGLAND*.

REFERENCES

1. Livingstone, Karen A. Science, art & industry : the work of William Burton, Gordon Mitchell Forsyth and Pilkington's Tile and Pottery Company in context in *Ars Ceramica* no.13 1996. p.67
2. Art : its effect upon the pottery industry in *Pottery Gazette and Glass Trade Review* 1st August 1921. p.1219
3. Cross, A.J. Pilkington's *Royal Lancastrian Pottery and Tiles*. Richard Dennis, 1980.
4. Livingstone. Op. cit.
5. Eatwell, Ann. Gordon Mitchell Forsyth (1879-1952) - artist, educator and father of art education in the Potteries in *Journal of the Decorative Arts Society* no.13 1989. p.27
6. Letter from Stanley Baldwin, 10 Downing Street, London, to Gordon Forsyth, 5 Oxford Terrace, Basford Park, 17th May 1928 [in Potteries Museum & Art Gallery archives]
7. Art instruction in the Potteries in *Pottery Gazette and Glass Trade Review* 2nd May 1927. p.815
8. Eatwell. Op. cit.

9. Haggar, Reginald. Bullers in *Northern Ceramic Society Echoes and Relections*, 1980. p.21

10. Ruscoe, William. *A Potter's Lot*. Unpublished autobiography. c.1982

11. Progress in ceramic art in *Pottery Gazette and Glass Trade Review* 2nd June 1930. p.974

12. Forsyth, G.M. Art education in the Potteries: a manufacturers' forward movement in *Pottery and Glass Record* February 1921. p.120

13. Rowland, Anna. Business management at the Weimar Bauhaus in *Journal of Design History* v.1 (3-4). 1988 p.153

14. Exhibition of British Industrial Art in Relation to the Home. Catalogue. June 20th - July 12th 1933.

15. Ruscoe, William. Op. cit.

16. Batkin, Maureen and Atterbury, Paul. Art among the insulators: the Bullers Studio 1932-52. Catalogue of an exhibition at the Gladstone Pottery Museum, Stoke-on-Trent. 1977. p.25

17. Haslam, Malcolm. *William Staite Murray*. Crafts Council/Cleveland County Museum Service, 1984. p.64

18. Ruscoe, William. Op. cit.

19. Batkin. Op. cit. p.11

20. Forsyth, G.M. British art in British industry in *Journal of the Royal Society of Arts* 14 December 1934. p.104

21. Royal Academy. Exhibition of British Art in Industry. Catalogue. January-March 1935

22. Batkin. Op. cit. p.13

23. Exhibition at museum in *The Sentinel* 21st June 1938

24. Batkin. Op. cit. p.11

The Potteries Museum & Art Gallery

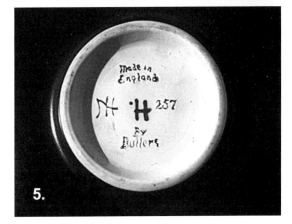

A selection of marks found on Bullers' art studio wares.

1. Anne Potts mark found on figures 1934-39.
2. Printed mark found on cast and thrown wares 1934-39.
3. Shortened impressed mark with shape number 1940-52.
4. Full impressed mark with glaze trial details 1940-52
5. Full impressed mark with shape number, AH for Agnete Hoy, H for Hilda Hine, 1944-52.

J Alcock

J Alcock

The construction of the Burlington Vase at Milton in the early 1930s. The workers are Fred Holmes (pattern maker), George Barnett (clay manager) and Charles Bettany (ceramist). The vase was exhibited in London but its eventual fate is unknown.

The completed vase showing the coat of arms of the Prince of Wales. The gentleman is Will Huyton, Ovens Manager.

Chapter 4

THE ART STUDIO UNDER AGNETE HOY

As demand for Bullers' electrical porcelain products continued throughout the hostilities of Second World War, the company were permitted full production, unlike many other domestic and decorative pottery companies in Stoke-on-Trent whose production was either halted by the government or "concentrated" within the manufacturing plant of another larger company. Under these circumstances, the production of artistic pottery as a sideline would have perhaps seemed an irrelevance and, indeed, inappropriate and so after the departure of Anne Potts the studio was effectively mothballed and the pottery which remained was left unheeded to gather dust in the studio. As it had not really been expected to generate income, no great financial loss was incurred from its closure.

Gordon Forsyth and the work of Burslem School of Art did, however, continue throughout this period as there was a constant demand for trained female staff in the pottery industry, particularly to replace those male operatives away at war. It was Forsyth who, once again, encouraged a restart of the Bullers' studio during this difficult social and economic period. Having seen that a studio could be made to work in an industrial setting, he would not have willingly abandoned the project on account of wartime exigencies.

AGNETE HOY

A young Danish potter named Agnete Hoy was visiting her family in England when war broke out. She had to remain in England and so she had to find employment to support herself, whilst also wishing to make a useful contribution to the war effort. Hoping to make use of her prior potting experience she contacted Wedgwood where their designer Victor Skellern recommended that she contact Gordon Forsyth to ask for his advice and assistance in finding suitable work within the pottery industry. On hearing of her training at Copenhagen School of Art and subsequent experience of working in a Danish country pottery and then in studios producing stoneware and porcelain, he immediately recommended her to Bullers as a suitable replacement for Anne Potts.

Hoy had first become interested in pottery through learning enamel painting on pottery as a hobby at evening classes in Denmark. At art school she specialised in pottery which was considered unusual for a woman in that school. She finished college in 1936 and went to work first in a country pottery and then in Gerhard Nielsen's pottery.

Agnete Hoy's own description of Forsyth's initial approach to Bullers does suggest that he was somewhat "economical" with the truth in terms of her experience, implying to Bullers (against her wishes) that she had worked for the Royal Copenhagen porcelain company. Bullers agreed to a trial period during which Hoy would produce some pieces at Burslem School of Art which would then be taken to Milton for firing and, if these proved acceptable, they agreed that the studio could possibly be reopened. All went according to plan and in 1940 Agnete Hoy found herself in sole occupancy of the studio just as it had been left after Anne Potts' departure.

Agnete Hoy Collection Archive

Agnete Hoy in the Bullers' studio.

Hoy described her experience of the reopening of the studio at Milton in recorded interviews made in 1998.[1] One of her first tasks was to create a suitable working environment and to do this she cleared out the studio including the work which had been left to gather dust in the intervening period. To this end, she held a sale within the factory of all the pots which were there and, to the surprise of the management, this generated some income and made them realise that she was serious about the venture. Her early trial days had been unpaid and so she now felt justified in asking for a wage, which turned out to be £6 per week.

Life in wartime Milton must have seemed rather bleak to Agnete Hoy. She had been brought up in a middle class home with staff such as a cook, parlourmaid, nanny and gardener. She was used to life in a comparatively rural environment and, prior to the war, had enjoyed the freedom of country life in Denmark. When she first came to work in Bullers she lodged in Baddeley Green with the cook from the Bullers' canteen and her duties as lodger included carrying in the coal and collecting what was known as the "supper beer". She liked sleeping with the window open but found it so cold here in the winter that she had to jump up and down in the bedroom to get warm and then sleep with extra clothes on.

In an interview she also recalled how cold it was in the morning in the early days of the studio. She was stirring the cold glaze with her hands and picking up cold pottery and this eventually gave her dreadful chilblains. Her hands were in such a mess that John Harris sent her to hospital for treatment. Once a dipper was brought in he showed her that the glaze should be stirred with a wooden paddle rather than immersing your hands in the solution.

To assist her in developing the studio a small team was assembled which combined youth with experience. Once again, Gordon Forsyth was involved in the selection of staff, recommending those whom he felt could ensure the success of the venture. Although Hoy was herself a competent thrower he suggested Harold Thomas as the main thrower and turner

Agnete Hoy in the Bullers' studio.

having already worked with him at both Pilkington's Royal Lancastrian Pottery, Manchester and at Burslem School of Art where Harold Thomas taught part-time. An experienced dipper named Fred Handley, who had worked at Simpson's of Cobridge was employed, and later other young apprentices were recruited from Burslem School of Art as and when required. Factory staff were also called upon to contribute advice as appropriate. Guy Harris was, as before, the source of the glazes used by the studio, whilst kiln men such as Albert Webb provided advice on the firing of the wares in the industrial ovens. A German (refugee) scientist called Dr. Bloch worked with Guy Harris at the time and he is believed to have also provided some technical assistance.

To begin with the team was necessarily small. Much of the initial work was of an experimental nature and, as previously, was supported by Bullers with no obvious financial return. With such a high level of experience amongst the group it must have been an artistically and technically rewarding environment. It is clear that Gordon Forsyth was actively involved in the studio during this 'middle' period as pieces survive which were signed and dated by him in the years around 1940. These include celadon glazed and crackle glazed wares. He acted as a mentor to Agnete Hoy who, as an already experienced potter, did not require instruction in basic pottery skills but learned new techniques from him such as how to carve into the leather hard clay in an oriental style and how to make appropriate tools for this work.

Initially, Hoy set herself the task of designing cookware - what would now be termed oven-to-table ware. Her own interests and experience were in the broad area of thrown vessel forms, so this was an application with which she felt comfortable and believed could have commercial possibilties. It was also suitable for production under wartime regulations as it was not classed as decorative but was of a utilitarian nature. She perceived that Bullers' high-fired porcelain was suitable for direct heating on cooking appliances and saw this development as innovative work in keeping with modern living and technological change. The resulting products were manufactured throughout the life of the studio and were displayed at several important exhibitions. Many are still in use today in the modern kitchen.

A commercial opportunity presented itself to the studio at an early stage. Heal's of

London expressed an interest in marketing Bullers' ware as they sold goods from other craft-based enterprises such as the Leach and Lamorna potteries in Cornwall. Their salesman, Harry Trethowan, was always on the lookout for new productions such as these as they had opened a department in their store entitled Heal's Craftsman's Market. In it they sold craft produced items which they claimed guaranteed the highest standards of quality in comparison to industrially produced items.[2] It is probable that Gordon Forsyth had introduced the Bullers' name to Trethowan as they were both active members of the Design and Industries Association. It has also been suggested that Harry Trethowan met Guy Harris when he was visiting the Stoke-on-Trent Rotary Club to talk about the manufacture of goods for the overseas market.

Agnete Hoy was invited to London to show Heal's her wares and took with her three barrels with a selection of her celadon glazed pots and oven-to-table ware which had been newly produced. Being rather proud of these new designs she was somewhat dismayed to find that they were not really what Heal's required. Although they liked the pots Heal's really wanted a range of animal figures suitable for their export markets. Having no prior experience of modelling or sculpting Hoy reluctantly agreed to attempt some animal figures. These were successfully manufactured (although never to Hoy's own taste) and advertised by Heal's in their mail order catalogues for several years.[3]

The contract with Heal's occasioned the employment of a young student from Burslem School of Art called James Rushton as modeller. One of his initial tasks was the casting of the Heal's animal figures and the modelling part was the production and sticking on of their ears, tails, eyelashes and other parts. Heal's catalogues show that they did also sell the other products of the studio and a verbal agreement is said to have existed with Heal's agreeing to sell everything produced by the Bullers' studio.

With this commercial backing the studio was able to expand further employing additional decorators and an apprentice thrower, Tony Morley, another recruit from Burslem. The experienced staff passed on their skills and Hoy herself encouraged staff to develop their own artistic talents whist herself retaining the final decision on what would be fired and sold, and always using the AH mark on studio productions with occasionally the painted mark of another decorator also present.

THE STUDIO ENVIRONMENT

Photographs of the studio depict a brightly lit, tranquil and organised environment. Examples of the wares produced were displayed on shelves around the studio. A sketch by Agnete Hoy shows the view over the surrounding countryside from the studio window. It was housed separately from the main factory, above the slip house in a room overlooking the canal. Workers from the main factory seem to have been generally unaware of the presence of the studio, apart from those who had day to day dealings with the staff there, such as the men supplying the studio with clay and glazes, the kiln men and ancillary workers such as packing staff, plumbers and electricians. Those who did have occasion to visit it commented on the contrast between the quiet environment there and that of the main factory floor.

Although Hoy was in charge of the studio work and the staff there, a fairly relaxed working regime appears to have pervaded. The older workers such as Harold Thomas and

The display area at Bullers' art studio c. 1948.

Agnete Hoy Collection Archive

View from art studio window looking towards Milton. Sketch by Agnete Hoy.

Agnete Hoy Collection Archive

Fred Handley would not have required or expected close supervision and one must imagine that they were treated as equals by Hoy because of their knowledge and skills. The more menial tasks fell to the junior staff such as Tony Morley and James Rushton who were expected to light the stove and collect clay from the factory. Some of the more unpleasant tasks were shared equally, such as stirring the cold glaze on winter's mornings, as Agnete Hoy felt that Mr Handley was too old to endure this task on his own - he worked there from the age of 57 to 69. She herself complained of chilblains from the cold work.

Fred Handley and children, Harry, Doug and Marjorie, c. 1946.

A Handley

However, all the staff were encouraged to develop their talents and to experiment with new ideas and techniques. Saturday morning was a day of work but on that morning and during the lunch hours the less experienced staff had the opportunity to try their hand at throwing or decorating and if the results met with Hoy's approval she would have the pieces fired and credit would be duly given to the makers.

One of the longest serving artists at the studio was James Rushton who had been Agnete Hoy's first apprentice. Having started at Bullers after Burslem School of Art in the role of

Heal's publicity photograph 1942.
Porcelain gazelles designed by Agnete Hoy.

Heal's

modeller, Rushton's artistic talents were noted both by Alan King who taught Rushton in the evenings at Stoke School of Art and by Agnete Hoy. After he had worked as her assistant for

Emmanuel Bah demonstrating the production of a pot by the coiling method.

Elsie Forrester 1942

James Rushton at work in the studio

Tony Morley, apprentice thrower in the art studio.

three years, Hoy recommended to John Harris that, having successfully gained a scholarship, the company should sponsor his attendance at the Royal College of Art in London. That they agreed to this does suggest that a long-term future for the studio was envisaged. The course was three years long and during this period Rushton received a guinea a week from Bullers to supplement his scholarship grant of £150 a year.[4] This was a reasonable sum when one considers that Rushton's colleague Tony Morley was being paid £1 10 shillings per week whilst working full time for the studio.[5]

Whilst at the Royal College between 1946-1949 Rushton studied ceramics under Professor Bobby Baker but also enrolled in the painting classes, as painting had always been his real interest, one which has continued to this day. After the three years were completed he returned to Bullers as he felt that he owed them a debt of gratitude and found that in his absence little had changed. He brought with him some new ideas for the studio and these will be mentioned later in the chapter.

Two women also worked in the studio as decorators and they frequently signed their wares. They were Elsie Forrester (1940-1952) and Hilda Hine (1944-1952). Their styles of decoration were similar to that of Agnete Hoy - they learned many techniques from her. Hilda Hine had been a student at Burslem School of Art and continued to decorate and exhibit her work locally after the studio closed.[6]

There were many short-term working visitors to the studio and although there to learn about the porcelain body and glazes each of them must have made their own contribution to the work. One such notable visitor was Michael Leach, son of the studio potter Bernard Leach. Bernard Leach had visited Bullers on a few occasions and perhaps felt that the experience of working there would be of more benefit to his son than working in a commercial tableware factory. Michael brought with him a background of working in stoneware in a small studio pottery in St Ives. The ware he produced at Bullers included mugs, bowls, cookware and teapots, some banded in blue. These pieces are stamped with his initials 'M.L.' or, more suprisingly, with the full Bullers' mark with his initials replacing those of Agnete Hoy. Apparently many of his pieces remained in the factory after he had left - perhaps they had not been of interest to Heal's. Both Leach and Chris Ludlow came to Bullers after the war, in 1947, on an ex-service retraining scheme.[7]

Chris Ludlow had worked for Heal's in London before becoming a pottery and glass retailer in St. Ives. He and Derek Wilshaw used their experience of working at Bullers to set up a pottery at Lamorna in Cornwall, around 1948, where Ludlow did most of the decorating and brushwork. At this time James Rushton was studying in London and he spent some of his vacation time helping them to establish the pottery. In a 1950 article Ludlow expressed his gratitude to John Harris of Bullers for his help and encouragement.[8] An ex-colleague of Wilshaw and Ludlow remembers their products as being technically more advanced than many of the other Cornwall studio potters. Their well-finished goods were considered too commercial by many of their Cornish contemporaries but perhaps this was a reflection of the experience they had brought from Bullers coupled with Ludlow's experience in the retail trade. Ludlow's Lamorna Pottery closed due to financial difficulties around 1952 but still exists today under different ownership.[9]

Other students spent varying lengths of time at Bullers and all moved on to follow different paths in potting. Robert Jefferson worked there to earn some extra money whilst a National Diploma student at Burslem School of Art studying under James Rushton. Jefferson had gone to Burslem after completing his National Service and had already studied at Liverpool College of Art. He was able to use his experience at Bullers, and some of the pottery that he made there, to obtain a place at the Royal College of Art in 1951. After various positions he returned to Burslem School of Art as a lecturer in ceramics. In 1958 he became the chief designer at Poole Pottery and there developed new ranges of tablewares featuring innovative decorative techniques. Echoing the Bullers experience he established a studio within the factory producing artistic wares and as late as 1964 launched a range of hand-thrown and hand-painted designs.[10]

Emmanuel Bah and Rosemary Wren produced some work at Bullers but little is known of their activities there. A fine figure attributed to Emmanual Bah is in the collection of the Potteries Museum & Art Gallery in Stoke-on-Trent. He is reported as returning to Jamaica after his time at Bullers[11] and may have been a visiting student placed with Bullers by Gordon Forsyth. However, another source refers to him as a Nigerian student placed at Bullers by Heal's.[11A]

Forsyth's daughter Moira also appears to have carried out some work at Bullers in co-operation with William Ruscoe. In his autobiography, Ruscoe recalled visiting the 1977 exhibition of Bullers' work at the Gladstone Pottery Museum. *"There were two exhibits which I had modelled and a Mother and Child designed by Moira Forsyth; this I well recalled modelling the features and the pleasure it gave me as I slowly developed it three dimensionally from the small drawing supplied by Miss Forsyth."*[12] Little of this work appears to have been produced and may even have been privately commissioned.

Other studio potters who visited the works included Katherine Pleydell-Bouverie, Nora Braden, Paul Barron, Heber Matthews and Henry Hammond (later to work with Agnete Hoy at Farnham College) but there is no suggestion that they produced any work there although many tried their hand at throwing the difficult porcelain body.

Local artist and designer Reginald Haggar decorated several pieces at Bullers in the mid-1940s, many of which were thrown (and signed) by Harold Thomas. After six years as Art Director at Mintons, Haggar was from 1934-1941 Head of Stoke School of Art and then from 1941-1945 was Head of Burslem School of Art. In 1934, with Gordon Forsyth, he had founded the Society of Staffordshire Artists and this acquaintance with Forsyth no doubt led to his employment in the local art schools and his work at Bullers. Haggar also researched and wrote extensively on the history of pottery and owned several important collections of pottery, now in the collection of the Potteries Museum & Art Gallery.[13]

A review of the staff of the studio would not be complete without mention of Harold Thomas and his skill as a thrower and also as a turner. He was able to work with the porcelain body more successfully than most others and could reduce its heaviness by turning back the thrown form. Such was his skill that for many years he was in demand as a demonstrator, particularly for foreign visiting parties or dignitaries to the Potteries, using the Wedgwood wheel which was at one time in Burslem School of Art and is now housed in the local museum. For these demonstrations he would call upon certain trusted acquaintances such as James Rushton to turn the wheel whilst he produced interesting novelty pieces for the visitors such

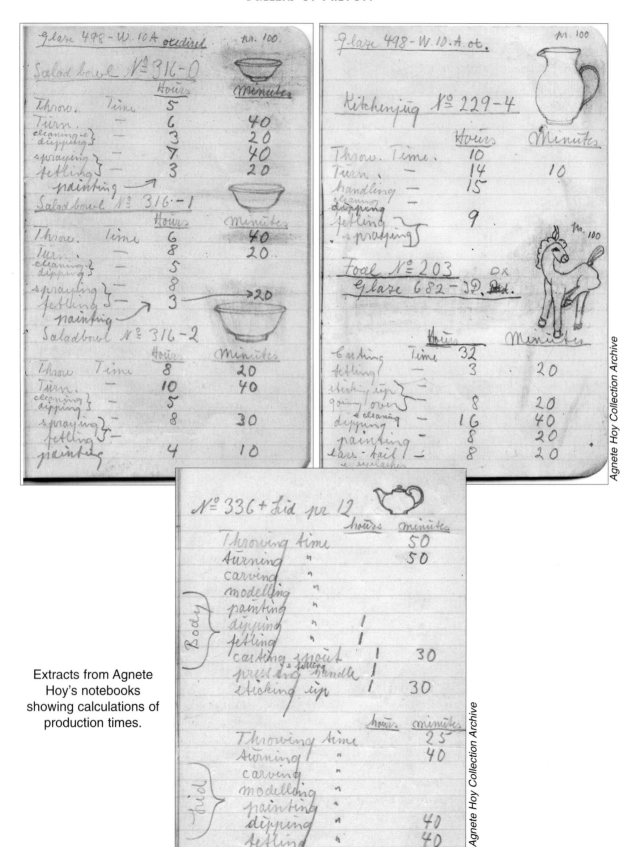

Extracts from Agnete Hoy's notebooks showing calculations of production times.

Agnete Hoy Collection Archive

118

as a teapot with perfect fitting lid and a pottery pork pie.

He worked at Bullers in the mornings and taught at Burslem School of Art in the afternoons. He found employment for some of his pupils, such as Tony Morley, at Bullers, and encouraged them to make use of his wheel when he was not using it. Once an Agnete Hoy design was established as a production item, Harold Thomas would make a slate template upon which further pieces could be based. It would be fair to say that the studio probably became too dependent upon his speed and skill, and when he decided to leave there was no strategy in place to fill the gap. Although some mechanisation of production had been discussed no action had been taken to ensure that this happened.

As a rule Harold Thomas did not sign the Bullers pieces as the decorators did. However, there are one or two unusual large vases which do bear his incised signature and date along with those of the decorator. It may be that these were actually thrown at Burslem

Harold Thomas.

School of Art rather than in the studio at Bullers. Harold Thomas was a Fellow of the Worshipful Company of Turners and was awarded their Silver Medal in 1934[13A].

STUDIO PRODUCTS

The studio productions all used the electrical porcelain body. The glazes were based on insulator glazes with adaptations by Guy Harris. It was this use of industrial materials which attracted the attention of the writers and art critics of the time such as Herbert Read and Nikolaus Pevsner. Read visited Bullers just after Agnete Hoy's arrival there and admired the work emerging from the kiln. Hoy remembered Guy Harris being gratified that their work was highly thought of by such a prominent figure from London. By all accounts, it received little local publicity except amongst the art school fraternity.

Shapes were numbered (usually a three digit number) and these numbers formed part of the markings on the base. The glazes were also numbered in a similar manner, the numbers reflecting the original insulator glaze. These glaze numbers were not normally included in the markings but occasionally it is possible to find a trial piece with some additional numbers and letters which may include this glaze number.

Agnete Hoy kept notebooks in which some of the shape numbers were noted alongside a small sketch. However, no complete catalogue of the studio products is known to exist. She calculated costs in this notebook in the same way as the insulator pattern books - each step in the production process being separately costed.

The later studio products almost always bear a standard impressed mark comprising AH with the shape number and *Made in England by Bullers*. Other painted or incised decorator's marks may be added to this - EF (Elsie Forrester), H or HMH (Hilda Hine), ML (Michael Leach), JR (James Rushton), HT (Harold Thomas), LW (Leslie West), GMF (Gordon Forsyth), RGH (Reginald Haggar).

Cookware

A range of cookware was produced from 1946 onwards and continued in production throughout the life of the studio. It was available in dark brown or in buff and decorated with brown bands of iron pigment. The range included egg poachers, nested casseroles with and without lids, one handled saucepans, bowls and jugs. They were heavy items designed to withstand daily kitchen use and, whilst not perhaps as elegant as some more modern oven to table wares they were truly practical and offered a more decorative alternative to the more commonly used Pyrex glass versions of the day. Their style was such that they would not look out of place in the kitchen of today.

The cookware was fired in an oxidising atmosphere in the tunnel kiln at around 1240° along with the insulators. This process was a 36 hour cycle. Although the decoration of these wares was not artistically challenging, all the studio artists worked on them when a batch was required. Skill was needed to ensure that everyone applied the same amount of pigment, otherwise the bands would have emerged from the kiln in different shades of brown.[14]

Although not favoured by Heal's for their export market (perhaps because of weight considerations), the cookware was exhibited at the 1946 *Britain Can Make It* Exhibition and again at the 1951 *Festival of Britain*. [see Appendix 4] The 1946 exhibition was the brainchild of Sir Stafford Cripps, President of the Board of Trade, who wanted to show the British public that new and exciting items would soon be available for them to purchase after the restrictions of the utility goods scheme. Bullers exhibited 28 items by Agnete Hoy, some of which were stated to be available for purchase immediately for both home and overseas markets.[15]

At the 1951 *Festival of Britain*, Bullers exhibited in the 'Country' Pavilion, along with studio potters such as Lucie Rie, Hans Coper, Bernard Leach, and Michael Cardew.[16] At the exhibition a leading U.S. retailer, Macy's, expressed an interest in buying these wares but Bullers were unable to meet their request because of their prior agreement with Heal's who claimed a monopoly on Bullers' products. At the time of the Festival, plans were afoot at Milton to mechanise production of these wares which at that time were still being individually thrown by Harold Thomas. It was felt that some shapes would be suitable for jolleying, leaving time for the artists to concentrate on new and more decorative products. A new extension was being built to the factory at Milton and space was to be found in the extension for this new production. Agnete Hoy and her staff believed that this would ensure a stable future for the studio.

Animals

We have already noted that the animal models were produced in response to a request from Heal's rather than by choice. Agnete Hoy did not like them[17]. Many other manufacturers, such as Denby, were also producing animal figures and Heal's advertised animals by Peggy

Foy in their catalogues alongside the Bullers' ones.[18]

The range included foal, camel, giraffe, calf, and gazelle and were sold for around 35/- to 65/- each (£1.75 - £3.25).[19] This was a substantial sum of money in the 1940s but we must remember that at this point in time they were only available for sale as export goods. Heal's advertised them in their 1942-1948 Wholesale and Export Division catalogues. It is possible that one of the reasons that Heal's liked them was because they were relatively easy to post overseas as mail order items. Their solid but stylishly modelled construction and matt glazing set them apart from other animal figures manufactured at the time just as it does today.

Although originally destined for export it is still possible to find examples of these in the U.K. Some may have been given to employees at the factory or have been bought at the closing down sale. Few remain intact as they were often given to children to play with and most have ears, antlers or tails which have proved susceptible to damage.

Some bird models were produced in addition to the range noted above, some lying in nests and glazed in celadons or matt black iron oxide.

Other modelled pieces were produced for the studio by William Ruscoe in the period 1941-1942. These were listed in his account book as a bull calf, and antelope and a girl seated, for each of which he was paid a fee of £3. In a letter dated 1979 he described the business arrangement as *"That I would have a free copy of each of these and that any other copies sold would yield a royalty of 5-10% (I cannot recall which) but as I did not ever receive any further money, I take it that none were sold."* [20] It is not known whether in fact any of these were produced, or if the modelled work was rejected.

Other decorative wares

The majority of the decorative wares produced by the studio took the form of vases and bowls. Many of the shapes were based on oriental forms - wide flat dishes which offered a large surface for decorative work and small rice bowls which, with their more vertical sides could show incised decoration both inside and out.

The colour palette used was not extensive. In the early days of the studio, when Anne Potts and Guy Harris were experimenting, a wider range of colours and glazes was in use. By this later period the studio team had developed a house style with less emphasis on glaze experimentation. The high firing temperatures and reducing atmosphere determined the nature of the decoration. These decorative wares were fired in a 200 saggar Davis kiln at around 1300 degrees. During the war only oxidised firings were permitted in the tunnel kiln, but after the war both oxidised and reduced firings were again carried out, reduced firings being especially for the studio wares as this was not appropriate for the insulators. All the wares were fired in saggars and most were placed on kiln furniture of the same body to keep them straight.[21]

The majority of pieces are decorated either with an iron rich pigment which gives shades of brown or with cobalt blue painted decoration on the white body. The celadon glazed wares display the incised or underglaze painted decoration to good effect and are either beige in colour from an oxidised firing or blue/grey from a reduction firing. Hoy's decoration flowed around the surfaces and shapes of the vessels. She believed that decorative work should not be too preconceived and described working on the pot as akin to composing music.

Much of the inspiration for the celadon glazed pieces was oriental, both in shape and decoration. A 1940 Gordon Forsyth bowl featured flowers carved in the style of the Sung potters of China. Agnete Hoy's work of this style was perhaps less derivative, her carved work on the oriental shapes being more abstract and free flowing. A lot of the celadon pieces are undecorated with the glaze alone complementing the shape.

Many of the decorative pieces were very small. These were often thrown by the apprentice staff and would have been used to fill gaps in the kiln between the larger items.

Few really large pieces appear to have been produced although Harold Thomas's throwing skills are evident on large storage jars decorated by Gordon Forsyth and vases decorated by Reginald Haggar. Decorated lamp bases were manufactured and were a popular line with customers of Heal's.

Later productions

Following his period of three years at the Royal College of Art, James Rushton returned to Bullers to find that relatively little had changed during his absence and the same shapes and designs were still being produced. Wishing to utilise the skill and inspiration that he had drawn from his period in London he introduced the technique of enamel painting to Agnete Hoy and the other studio staff. This style was in contrast to the muted colours of the standard productions and could have perhaps broadened the appeal of the studio products to a wider market.

There were some technical difficulties to be overcome to ensure that the overglaze decoration adhered to the glaze under the high firing conditions required for the porcelain body. The ware had to undergo a long period of 'soaking' after the firing and some very successful pieces started to be produced. These included a range of mugs and coffee pots with milk jugs and sugar basins, based on elegant 18th century shapes. The decoration was often a central motif of a flower or bird and both Agnete Hoy and James Rushton decorated these. As this type of decoration was more time consuming and therefore more expensive its continued production was based on the assumption that the ovenware would indeed be moved to industrial production methods such as jolleying leaving the artists more time to concentrate on the enamel painting.

THE CLOSURE OF THE STUDIO

As well as a small production unit within Bullers, the studio had for many years been an artistic meeting place for many people connected with Burslem School of Art. Gordon Forsyth, Reginald Haggar, Moira Forsyth and William Ruscoe all produced work for, or at, Bullers' studio, using the throwing skills of their part-time colleague Harold Thomas. Quite how some of this non-commercial work was viewed by the company management is not clear, nor do we know if any of these pieces ever found their way to Heal's. One must assume that the Harris family sanctioned these additional pieces of work, usually signed, as many of them did immediately pass into private ownership although some were also donated to the local museum. Many pieces also found their way into the local community via garden fetes and other events which were supported by the Harris family.

However, times and personalities had changed. The company management had undergone changes and the original supporters of the studio, such as Guy and Gilbert Harris, were less influential in the decision-making process. Harold Thomas had decided to return to full-time teaching, Fred Handley was in his 70s and about to retire, and Agnete Hoy had married and was now living in London, sending work back to Milton every fortnight via the company transport to be fired and only occasionally visiting the studio in person. Outside the company, the influence of Gordon Forsyth was lost - he had died in 1952 - and Heal's decided that they no longer wished to purchase goods from the studio.

This was a massive blow to the future of the studio. As Heal's were the only outlet for its productions another wholesaler would have had to be found to market the stocks which had been accumulating in the Joiner's Square store. The management saw no future in pursuing this venture and quite unexpectedly closed down the studio in March 1952. The news was broken to the staff by John Harris and they were given two weeks notice and two weeks pay. Tony Morley, by then the thrower, moved into a position as an insulator jolleyer in the main factory, whilst James Rushton took up a full time teaching position at Burslem School of Art.

The trade press reported the closure in May and noted that this was in spite of pieces from the studio selected for the *Festival of Britain* were to be included in the Design Review for permanent record.[22]

A sale of the remaining stock was held in the factory when the unsold goods were returned from Heal's and this was probably the first time that many of the workers had had the opportunity to see or buy the work of the Bullers' studio. The area where the studio had been was converted into additional laboratory space around 1953.

Agnete Hoy moved on to work for Doulton in Lambeth from 1952-1956 producing goods in saltglazed stoneware. She taught in several art colleges in London and the south of England but maintained contact with Bullers. When she brought groups of students on annual study visits to the potteries of Stoke-on-Trent she always visited the Milton factory and took away a supply of clay for the students to work with, echoing the initial contact between Bullers' industrial goods and the art schools.

Postscript

Bullers' facilities were once again used for the production of studio pottery in 1985-86 and 1990-91 when potter Jenifer Jones produced some large stoneware pots there. These were commissioned by the architects Powell and Moir. The first set of 6-foot high pots were for the Queen Elizabeth Conference Centre in London, for an outdoors courtyard, whilst the later ones were for the Conquest Hospital in Hastings. The pots were produced using coils of clay and they were fired in Bullers' tall kilns along with the insulators.

REFERENCES

1. National Electronic and Video Archive of the Crafts, University of the West of England. Anita Hoy. Series of interviews recorded in 1998
2. Heal's. Craftsman's Market leaflet. Heal's, 1948
3. Heal's. Cargo of presents for particular people. Heal's, 1946 (and other catalogues)
4. Interviews with James Rushton. 2000 and 2002
5. Letter from Tony Morley to Sue Taylor, January 2000
6. Batkin, Maureen and Atterbury, Paul. Art among the insulators: the Bullers Studio 1932-52. Catalogue of an exhibition at the Gladstone Pottery Museum, Stoke-on-Trent. 1977. p.

7. Ibid.

8. A venture in Cornish slipware in *Pottery Gazette and Glass Trade Review* May 1950. p.711

9. Interviews with James Rushton, 2000 and Bill Picard, 2001

10. Casey, Andrew. *20th Century Ceramic Designers in Britain*. Antique Collectors Club, 2001. Ch.16

11. Batkin. Op. cit. p. 25

11A. Handwritten note on reverse of photograph belonging to Albert Webb

12. Ruscoe, William. *A Potter's Lot*. Unpublished autobiography. c.1982

13. Catalogue. Reginald Haggar: retrospective exhibition of watercolours 1930-1980. City Museum & Art Gallery, 1980,

13A. Batkin. Op. cit. p. 27

14. Interview with James Rushton, 2002

15. Council of Industrial Design. *Britain Can Make It* exhibition catalogue. H.M.S.O., 1946

16. Niblett, Kathy. Ten plain years: the British pottery industry 1942-1952 in *Northern Ceramic Soc.J.* v.12 1995. p.175-213

17. NEVAC interview. Op. cit.

18. Heal's. Publicity leaflet. 1947

19. Heal's. Come to the Christmas Fair leaflet. 1947 (and others)

20. Letter from William Ruscoe to Pat Halfpenny 1st December 1979

21. Hoy, Anita. Art among the insulators in *Ceramic Review* no.69 1981 p.10-11

22. Notes and news in *Pottery and Glass* May 1952 p.89

J Alcock

The Bullers' art studio showing L to R, Chris Ludlow, Hilda Hine,
Derek Wilshaw and Harold Thomas 1946

Art pottery at Milton in 1986. The factory was occasionally used by studio potters. These vases by Jenifer Jones were destined for The Queen Elizabeth Centre, London.

Decorative wares sold through Heal's, London.

Heal's

Range of animal figures available
through Heal's

Chapter 5

MEMORIES OF BULLERS

The history of an enterprise such as Bullers would not be complete without reference to the experiences of some of the thousands of people who worked there. Here are a few memories.

IRIS JOHNSTON (NEE WOOD)

Mrs Iris Johnston worked at Bullers' Milton factory from 1940 until 1955. She worked in the testing department and then in the administrative offices. When she left school she had really wanted to work in a shop, or in an office, but her mother told her that a job had been found for her at Bullers by a family friend. She didn't want to go to work there, but she said that in those days you had to do what your parents told you to do.

She remembered the long working days before the war - from 8 a.m. until 5.50 p.m. - this was a 47 hour 40 min week. After the war, working conditions improved and the working week was reduced to 44 hours which meant that she didn't have to work on Saturday mornings any more. She was paid 12s 11d per week when she started work and when she finished in1955 this had risen to £5 per week.

There was a workers' canteen which had been built at the beginning of the war and once a week she enjoyed concerts which took place there when workers from the factory did a turn. There was also a cricket club and a football club.

Workers came to Milton from Baddeley Green, Norton, Smallthorne, Sneyd Green, Abbey Hulton, Bucknall and some even came from as far as Longton.

She remembered Mr Guy and Mr Gilbert Harris as Managing Directors when they were in their 60s. Mr Gilbert lost two sons in the war around 1940-1941 and the workers had a penny a week stopped out of their wages for several weeks to buy a cot for the North Staffordshire Royal Infirmary in memory of these two sons. She thought that this had purchased a bed and then paid for its upkeep. All the factory staff were very upset about their deaths, especially the older people.

When Gilbert Harris was in his 60s he would arrive about 9.30 am, and by 10.00 am, without fail, he walked through every department of the factory speaking to people. Looking back on this practice Mrs Johnston felt that it was a good thing for the management to do.

The department was very noisy. When the insulators were being tested it was like a thunder and lightning storm. Accidents occasionally happened and one lady was badly electrocuted and had to be taken to hospital but thankfully did recover. After this, safety was improved. Mrs Johnston dealt with the paperwork for orders for telephone insulators from as far afield as Iran and Iraq. She remembered instructions coming with an order stating that, when packed, the crates mustn't be too heavy as when they left the ship they would be carried by mules over the mountains. The foreman of the packing department was Mr George Hawthorne and he ruled with a rod of iron.

She believed that the advent of plastic materials was one of the reasons for the company eventually losing business, especially in the area of dust-pressed insulators. She pointed out that when you buy a plug nowadays it will be plastic rather than porcelain; that you no longer

I Johnston

The ladies of the testing department at Milton c. 1948. L to R Back: Betty Jones, Dorothy Deaville, Mary Keeling. Front: Iris Wood, Betty Sergeant, Gladys Marriatt (Osborne) and Margaret Ryles.

I Johnston

Ladies of the testing department enjoying a lunch break c.1950. L to R Lilian Woolridge (middle), Betty Sergeant (front), Iris Wood (back), Ann Foster (middle), Betty Jones (back), Joyce Deaville (front),

require strings of insulators on telegraph poles; and that where you used to have large transformers in residential areas using big insulators, these have now been reduced to a fairly compact box. This was the result of progress.

BILL DAVIES

Bill Davies worked as a plumber at Milton from 1939 until 1983, occasionally also looking after the plant on the other site at Hanley and later at Taylor Tunnicliff's Longton factory. His father had also been the company plumber and his three uncles were joiners and a grinder. When he was 14 years old he became his father's assistant. When he started work at the factory there were five plumbers.

The Davies family lived in the lodge house at the factory gates (now demolished). His father was required to go round the works every night at 8 p.m. to check that everything was well. In those days there was no fence round the factory and Mr Davies remembered the well-known Potteries tramp, Vincent Riley, occasionally going to sleep in the boiler house. (Apparently it was common practice for this tramp of no fixed abode to sleep in the ovens of various factories around the Potteries). Although he did no harm he had to be moved on if discovered. Eventually a fence was erected to prevent intruders gaining access.

Mr Davies recalled how strict the bosses were in those days and how you could be sacked at a moments notice for misdemeanours. The Works Manager at that time was Mr. Pennell and he used to come round on inspections feeling the gas rings to see if they were warm from workers having illicit cups of tea. One day he went into the joiner's shop and noticed something in the joiner's mouth. He thought it was a cigarette and was going to sack him on the spot - in fact it was only a wood shaving. As an apprentice, he was expected to leave the workshop if any of the managers came in to speak to his father. When he was about sixteen he used to pick apples in Mr Pennell's garden at Endon and was paid 2s 6d for this.

Mr. Davies told how he and the other tradesmen employed by Bullers were called out to the houses of the managers to effect repairs and install new appliances. Another perk for management was to have access to the company stores and he recalled them selecting decorated door knobs and finger plates from the catalogues for their houses. Occasionally he worked at Mr Pennell's house at Endon where he was told not to make any noise between 1.00 and 2.00 because that was when he had his afternoon nap. Mr Pennell sometimes came out to supervise this work at his home wearing a smoking jacket and smoking a cigar.

He described how the kiln men worked through the night and, when not doing their own work, rather than do nothing they would place the ware onto the kiln trucks ready for firing. They would also empty the trucks which came out of the kiln during the night so that they were really also acting as placers and emptiers. In the early days of Mr. Davies' employment another night-time worker was the man who shovelled the waste clay from the turning shop down a hole into the clay cellar. Horses and carts used to come and collect the clay and take it back to the slip house for recycling in the blungers. Later a moving belt was installed which took the clay away as it fell on the floor.

Mr Davies occasionally visited the art pottery studio to carry out work such as repairing the lead on the throwing tables. He told how workers would use the mugs produced in the studio for their tea. The studio was a very quiet place compared to the main works.

ALBERT BOOTH

Albert Booth went to work at Bullers aged around $14^1/_2$. He had worked at the Globe Pottery in Cobridge for five months as a mould runner but a job at Bullers was much nearer to his home in Abbey Road - he spent less time travelling to and from work and was not so tired after a day's work. He remembered he and his brothers falling asleep immediately after their evening meal because they were all so tired after a hard day's work.

He started work at Bullers the day after war broke out in 1939. He found a subdued atmosphere in the factory as many of the men were very apprehensive at the prospect of being called up and were clearly not themselves that day.

Bullers was a better place to work than the Globe Pottery. Although he worked a 48 hour week he had a 10 minute break at 10.00 am, forty minutes for lunch and a cup of tea at 3.00 pm which he was expected to drink while working. He worked on Saturdays from 8.00 am until 11 am. Sometimes in the lunch break he and some others would have a game of football by the canteen building or would sit out by the canal. On Fridays he collected his pay from the office but never opened his wage packet himself. He was expected, like others of his age, to take this home unopened to his father or mother who would give him pocket money from it and keep the rest for the housekeeping.

Although he started as a mould runner carrying two parts of an insulator to and from the drying room, the work he was asked to do at Bullers was more varied and he could see better prospects for his future career there. He was only a mould runner for about a year and then moved on to basic jolleying of setters (for placing the ware on during firing), grinding balls and then mortars and pestles. He was always called Tony at work, not Albert, because his supervisor thought that he looked Italian.

He remembered making thousands of mortars during his time at the factory. As a trainee boy he made small ones - sizes 0 -12. He had to do all the processes himself, jolleying the clay, cutting and shaping the foot, and finally stamping the words Warranted Acid Proof - the size number - Made in England - and then his own identification letter, which was D. This was to calculate his tally for piecework payment. Experienced staff could make 400 - 500 of the small sized mortars a day. He remembered Boots the Chemists being one of the main customers.

During the early years of the war he carried out fire watching duties during the night at the factory. A group of men were trained in fire fighting and used an old cricket shed on the works as their headquarters. This was kitted out with a couple of bunks and the older men used to let him go to sleep while they sat up playing cards during the long night. They then went to the factory canteen for a good breakfast before starting a normal working day. He remembered being paid 3 shillings for this extra work. A couple of big air raid shelters had been built on the works but sometimes it was quicker to go from the shop floor down into the tunnels under the works which carried the piping.

From 1943 to 1946 he was in the armed forces and when Bullers asked for his release he came back to work as a jolleyer. As he was now a more mature and skilled worker he remembered the manager deciding eventually that he should be paid as a journeyman, even although he had not completed the usual length of apprenticeship. He earned more as he progressed on to the more skilled task of 'sticking up' large shedded insulators and so he had been correct in forseeing a brighter future at Bullers.

Albert recalled the day he finally retired from Bullers. As a long-serving member of staff he was entitled to a farewell drinks party and a sandwich buffet with the management in the company offices to which he was allowed to invite twelve of his friends from the factory floor. There were no company pensions and so he received a cheque for £250 and had his photograph taken. He also had another retirement party with his workmates when he was allowed (against all the rules) to take some beer and whisky into the workshop. They had a good party and gave him hedge clippers and a camera to enjoy in his retirement.

Gift marks his half century of service

Mr. John Harris, Managing Director of Bullers Limited, Milton, presenting a cheque to Mr. George Hawthorne, who retired yesterday after 54 years' service. Mr. G. H. Harris (Chairman) is extreme left.

Newspaper photograph of the retirement of George Hawthorne, head of the packing warehouse in 1958 after 54 years of service. L to R, Gilbert Harris, Charles Bettany, John E. Harris, Ralph Berrisford, A. W. Jeffery, George Hawthorne, Nigel Harris, Jack Bonell and Fred Holmes.

JAMES SIMCOE

James Simcoe had worked as a miner before joining the Air Force where he did administrative work, which he enjoyed. He then worked on the railways before moving to Bullers at the age of 30, in 1950, where he was able to earn more money. When he first went on to the factory he remembered the smell, which he didn't like, but otherwise found it a clean and reasonable environment in which to work, compared to the mines. The company provided him with overalls and he took his own old shoes to wear at work.

When he started at Bullers he trained as a profile turner and remembered being trained by a young woman. As he had worked with women in the Air Force he did not find this unusual, and pointed out that it was quite common for women to carry out this task at Bullers if the pieces being made were not large. He thought the atmosphere of men and women working together was quite jolly and remembered the women singing along to "Workers'

Playtime" on the radio.

The workers at Bullers were very proud of their high level of skill. Mr Simcoe's immediate supervisor was George Brown. The boss was Jack Bonell who was strong on discipline but fair. His office was in the jolley shop and so he was not always present in the turning shop. He was also the manager of Northwich Victoria Football Club, and arranged employment at Bullers for several ex-players from the local football clubs - Stoke City and Port Vale - including Eddie Adams, Bob Meadows, Derek Mountford, Albert Mullard and Ray Askey.

In 1960 Mr. Simcoe left Bullers to go to G.E.C's Parkhall Pottery at the Sutherland Works in Longton before moving on to MacIntyres. When things didn't work out there he went back to see Jack Bonell who gave him a job back at Bullers and eventually sent him on a training course which enabled him to become a supervisor and trainer. Of all his jobs he had enjoyed working at Bullers most because of the people and the friendly atmosphere.

TONY BAILEY

Tony Bailey joined Bullers in 1965 as a trainee manager with the intention of attending college on a day-release basis during his training period. He remembered being left with one of the factory workers on the first day who informed him that he was on the "wrong side". As he could not understand what this meant, the man explained to him that he was wasting his time in management as he could be making more money on the factory floor doing piece work. When he collected his £6 wage at the end of the first week and compared this to what some of the men on piece work were earning, he understood why this had been said. A manager's wages could be perhaps only 2/3 of that of the operatives, but they had the benefit of paid sick leave whereas those on piece work were not paid if they did not work.

Starting in the jolley shop, he worked as an assistant to the Production Director and manager of the shop, Jack Bonell. The men who wielded the most power in the factory were the mould makers and the stickers-up, and they had to be dealt with diplomatically lest they should be offended. Their skills and experience were such that their occasional tantrums were tolerated by management.

He remembered the saggar maker, Ralph Whieldon, appearing on the television quiz show "What's My Line?" hosted by Eamonn Andrews. The celebrity panel could not guess his occupation which was given as "Saggar maker's bottom knocker", thus bringing this Potteries' occupation national recognition. Mr. Whieldon received a scroll which was proudly displayed at the works.

One dignitary he met whilst at Bullers was Anthony Armstrong-Jones, Lord Snowdon. He toured the works and caused some consternation when he decided to climb the ladder to talk to the sticker-up who was busy working at the top of an insulator. At least it seemed to indicate a genuine interest in what was being produced.

He described the staff at Bullers as being "engineers in clay", rather than potters, and the factory as a self-sufficient enterprise making all its own clay and employing all its own tradesmen - only raw materials were brought in. It was a good place to work and over the years he worked his way up through the ranks of management until in 1998 he became Production Director and was invited to join the Board.

JUNE ALCOCK

June Alcock started work as an office junior at Bullers in 1946. She had stayed on at Endon High School to learn shorthand and typing. She remembered that the Harris family were gentlemen and that when they ran the company it was a nice place to work. Her working day started by clocking in at 8.30 am whereas the factory workers started earlier, at 8.00 am. In her 40 minute lunch break she used the canteen at the back of the works where you could buy your lunch (known as "rice and ice") for 2 shillings.

She and other office staff participated in social events organised by the company as can be seen from the photographs of a variety show held in the Jubilee Hall.

Her father Albert Webb was the fireman between 1929 and 1959. He used to fire the old bottle ovens and then, as technology changed, he moved on to the gas and electric ovens. One of his particular responsibilities was the

J Alcock

J Alcock

Bullers' concert in the Jubilee Hall, Stoke c. 1956.
Above: L to R Charlie Taylor (Lodge Man), Russell Robbins, two staff transferred from the London Office, Charles Bettany on piano (Technical Manager).

Left: Skiffle group, and 'A Sweet Old-Fashioned Girl' starring, L to R, Graham Mitchell, Charlie Taylor, Walter Tutty, ? Russell Robbins, Margaret Foreman, June Webb, Harry Wright.

firing of the ware from the art pottery studio. When Mr. Webb started at Bullers, Bill Huyton was in charge of the ovens department but over the years the managers of this department included Arthur Walker, Jack Benton, Stan Sharp and Charles Skellam. Albert Webb worked at Bullers until he was 69 years old. He worked nights and at weekends - when the kilns were being fired, he would have to go to the factory. If the family had all been out for the evening he would always call in at the works on his way home to take kiln readings, even as late as midnight. Of course, no overtime was paid for these trips. She described it as "My dad never left Bullers".

Those working in the offices were very poorly paid and earned less than the girls on the factory floor who could earn more money by working piece work.

J Alcock

Albert Webb's retirement 1959. L to R, Donald Harris, Stan Sharp (Ovens Manager), Harry Bishop (Electrician), Albert Webb (Foreman), Ron Brandreth (Assistant Electrician)

MARGARET HANCOCK (NEE FOREMAN)

Margaret Hancock worked in the administrative offices with June Alcock. She remembered a representative from Bullers coming to Endon High School towards the end of each school year to recruit girls with shorthand and typing skills. At her interview in 1951 she recalled being told to take her hands out of her pockets - she had kept them there because she was so nervous. She described the company as very family orientated but as paying poor wages. In spite of the wages people stayed there for their whole working lives, but by the late 1950s people had started to leave for jobs in other factories which paid better wages.

Margaret Hancock and her friend both lived at Stanley and in the summer they cycled to work at Milton every day. She was disappointed when her friend was transferred to Bullers'

Hanley works and had to catch a bus to Hanley. The bike shed at the works was full of bikes, as most local people cycled to work.

The clay was delivered at least four or five times a day. Her job entailed taking paperwork and samples round different departments on the works, from the press shop to the fettler and to the jolleyer, so she got to meet lots of different people. She worked at Bullers for 39 years. In the later years there were problems with the supply of metal fittings from the Tipton works. This caused delays in meeting customer orders and the Progress and Production Manager Alan Jeffery was having to ask clients to wait 6 to 8 weeks for delivery.

Discipline was strict. She remembered a man being sacked when a small team of men were carrying a newly completed bushing insulator using heavy straps and it toppled over. One of the men laughed and joked about it. One of the managers instantly called him over and sacked him for treating such an expensive loss as a laughing matter.

She went to the sale of art pottery when Bullers' studio closed in 1952 when she was 16 years old. No-one seemed too impressed by what they saw. People didn't have much money to spend on such extras and there were no collectors around in those days. She herself only had 2s 6d pocket money but bought an Agnete Hoy Bambi model.

She used Milton Brook pottery in her kitchen at home for many years. It was more expensive than other similar dishes, costing maybe three times as much as other manufacturers' products, but she believed that it produced better results in cooking.

Bullers had a big social club and the tickets for their dances were sold out before they were printed. Some dances were held at the King's Hall in Stoke. At the factory the social club had table tennis and there was also a tuck shop. She also remembered a variety show in the Jubilee Hall in Stoke.

GRAHAM BELL

Graham Bell worked in the laboratory at Bullers from 1953 and was taken on by Guy Harris, who was his first boss. His job entailed testing the clay body and glazes for insulators. When he started as a laboratory assistant, placing the trials, his pay was £3 7s 6d. After Guy Harris retired, the company chemist in the 1950s was Reg Batchelor and then in the early 60s he was replaced by Charles Bettany.

He recalled that the glaze recipe book, being of value, was kept in the safe and when a new batch of glaze was needed, handwritten notes were made from this book by an assistant and these were taken onto the works.

After they had stopped using horses, a tractor was used in the factory for pulling the carts carrying away the scrap clay. Mr Bell remembered the driver was a chap called George Barlow who used to go to the Co-op in Baddeley Green for his groceries. These he would put in a sack from Bullers which had once contained feldspar. He lived in Baddeley Green in a cottage with two doors and to clean his cottage he would take a bucket of water and throw it through from one door out the other. On one occasion, Port Vale supporters were travelling to London to watch their team play Leyton Orient in a cup tie. When the Bullers' contingent assembled at Cobridge Station for the excursion train to the match they were horrified to see George arrive straight from work, dressed in his clogs, jacket tied around the waist with a rope (no buttons), and his cap covered in clay dust. George's parents owned the wharf rights on the canal. There were rumours that he had a lot of money buried somewhere.

Although they had to work long night shifts, Mr Bell remembered that some of the kiln men put this time to good use. When dawn broke sometimes they would go gathering mushrooms in the fields next to the factory. The kiln area was also a convenient place to dry the family laundry overnight whilst no supervisors were around to notice.

Mr Bell remembered Agnete Hoy from her annual return visits to Bullers with groups of students and described her as a flamboyant character wearing lots of taffeta skirts. On one of her visits he and his colleagues took her round to the Victoria Pub where she enjoyed a pint of beer.

JIM KNOX

Jim Knox started work in the Bullers' garage in 1949 aged 14^1/$_2$ as an assistant to the foreman Arthur Mellor. They would service and clean the company cars which belonged to the managers, including an old Aston Martin, a Humber Snipe and Mr Jeffery's Vauxhall. By that time there was no chauffeur and the managers drove themselves. He recalled that, on a bad day, Arthur would find as many as ten or twelve cars to be cleaned, usually on a Friday!

Jim Knox's father had spotted the advert for the vacancy at Bullers and sent his son down to the works to apply for the job. When he started, his weekly wage was £1 2s 6d. When he went home with this wage packet his mother took the £1 and gave him back 2s 6d. At Christmas everyone got a Christmas bonus, probably something like £3.

The garage staff had the same hours as the factory workers. On a Saturday they worked from 8.00 am until 1.00 pm and during this time they worked on cars belonging to other staff (who did not use company cars) such as the Riley 9 belonging to Mr. Twist the lodgekeeper. A nearby farmer also used to avail himself of the facilities in exchange for some bacon (at that time rationed), which was then cooked on the garage coke stove. The management appeared to turn a blind eye to these Saturday repairs. Occasionally, one of the Harris family would purchase a second-hand car and Jim and Arthur would be tasked with its renovation, from the removal of much rust right through to the application of up to ten coats of paint.

Jim Knox himself cycled to work. Arthur Mellor used to send him on his bicycle to Hanley and Burslem to get spare parts for the cars which were being repaired. He recalled that one day he cycled into the back of another vehicle and had to be taken to the local doctor, a Dr. Glass. He went back to work but his bike was broken. John Harris heard of the accident and gave him ten shillings to have his bike repaired.

He recalled that the horses which worked on the factory were originally stabled on Bullers' land, beside the canal. Later they were moved to George Bartlam's farm across the road from the main entrance. Farmer Bartlam's two sons worked at Bullers.

JAMES RUSHTON

James Rushton enrolled at Burslem School of Art on 3rd February 1942. The headmaster of the School, Mr Johnston, told the pupils that there was a job at Bullers for a modeller. James Rushton really wanted to be a painter but there was no opportunity for him to do this and so he applied for the job at Bullers. He was interviewed by Agnete Hoy and he remembered taking with him a portfolio of life drawings to show her.

His mother was pleased that his job allowed him to wear a white collar and tie rather than being a dirty job at the clay end of a pottery factory.

His first duties in the Bullers' studio included fetching the sandwiches from the canteen and stoking up the coal stove which heated the studio. His journey to the canteen entailed going through the factory and running the gauntlet of the women in the pressing shop who mercilessly tormented a young 15 year old - something which he came to dread.

In the studio he cast animal models and modelled small parts for the animals such as eyelashes and tails. Eventually he learned how to decorate with the brush and to throw on the wheel. He believed that his situation in the studio was an excellent apprenticeship; he learned many different skills, unlike some other young pottery workers.

He remembered Gilbert Harris as a very kind patriarchal figure coming round the factory every morning talking to people. When he visited the art pottery studio he would see pieces which he liked and would take them for his charitable jumble sales and garden parties, sometimes to the chagrin of the artists who had made them. He described the atmosphere in the studio as very easy-going, with students and other artists coming and going, apparently with the blessing of the Harris family.

JENIFER JONES

Studio potter Jenifer Jones worked at the Milton factory on two occasions, 1985 and 1990-91, both times to make large pots which had been commissioned for new buildings - the Queen Elizabeth II Conference Centre in Westminster and the Conquest Hospital, Hastings. She was recommended to approach Allied Insulators by B.C.R.A. as they had kilns of a suitable size and which could fire to the required temperature. Her stay there was arranged by the production manager Frank Riley who made some studio pottery himself in his spare time.

J Jones

A space was found for her to work in the big bushing shed, at the far end of the site. This was a large and purpose-built and was where the largest insulators were made, and where driers, spray booths and kilns for these large pieces were kept. Jenifer found the workforce highly skilled; she felt that the men here were probably the elite of the workforce.

In 1985 there were around 12-15 men working there, with three work stations for making the sections along one wall, and two for the joining of the sections on the opposite side. In the middle the sections were all laid out to dry in their plaster moulds. The finished insulators were lined up on the end wall to dry, 20 feet high, a splendid sight, she remembers.

Jenifer worked next to Ernie Banner and his assistant Albert. She found them very friendly and helpful as they explained the factory routine, helped her to set up her work station and generally looked after her. She found the whole factory atmosphere very friendly with everyone on first name terms and little status distinction.

When she returned to the factory for her second visit she did notice that there were less people working in the bushing shed and there were rumours of not enough orders, and competition from Japan.

Bullers' Milton works had excellent transport facilities, with canal, railway and road all adjacent. The chimneys of the factory can be seen beyond the road bridge.

MILTON STATION.

Chapter 6

BULLERS' LATER ACTIVITIES

Throughout its existence the company concentrated on the manufacture of insulators and associated products. However some later product ranges were developed alongside these, in addition to the studio wares.

When the art pottery studio was abruptly closed it was suggested to its redundant staff that it would hopefully be a temporary measure and that the planned production of their cookware range would be restarted. This never happened, but several years after its closure a new product range started by the then Chairman Alan Lloyd was introduced under the trade name Milton Brook Pottery. This venture was operated under the umbrella company of A.I. Ceramic Products Ltd.[1] and was based in a separate part of the factory. The name may have been created from an amalgamation of the names of the nearby villages Milton and Stockton Brook. The range of products included flan and casserole dishes, mortars and pestles (which had been manufactured since the company started in Hanley in the 19th century) and other small items such as egg coddlers.

The design of the mortars and pestles had not changed over the years but for the Milton Brook range they were also produced with colourful glazes such as yellow, green and blue on the mortars, in keeping with the décor of the modern kitchen. The upsurge in cookery as a leisure activity increased the demand for such products amongst housewives who had started to make more use of fresh herbs and spices. Products originally designed and produced by the company for industrial and scientific purposes became available for purchase in stylish hardware shops.

In 2001 these items were available from Wade's Milton Brook range in sixteen sizes, close to the range sold in the 19th century. Their literature stated:

"The Milton Brook range of mortars and pestles have been a long standing favourite for over a century. Their non-porosity and exceptional quality avoids any taste residue, odour or stain after washing. Available in a large variety of sizes, the mortars and pestles serve both the culinary and pharmaceutical markets."[2]

The casserole and baking dishes in the Milton Brook range differed radically from the studio wares of the 1940s and 1950s. They were industrially produced using automatic machines which also carried out the fettling process, and were spray glazed with a glossy finish, in contrast to the matt insulator glaze of the earlier pieces. The electrical porcelain body was still used. The range was available in plain white; Sandstone (yellow/brown); or Rockingham (dark brown). Lithographic floral decoration was also used on the white background.

In the 1970s a new type of casserole dish was briefly in vogue in the modern kitchen - the slow cooker. Bullers made these for a short time under the Milton Brook trade name but ceased production fairly quickly.

The success or otherwise of the Milton Brook Pottery venture is unclear. Some have reported the cookware products as unreliable owing to the nature of their design whilst other

REGD. OFFICE
MILTON
STOKE ON TRENT

Bullers Ltd.

TIPTON 1691 ext 14
BULLERS TIPTON
TIPTON or DUDLEY PORT [L M R]

MANUFACTURERS OF
DOOR FURNITURE · NAME PLATES ETC IN PORCELAIN & GLASS
BEER ENGINE HANDLES · TAP DISCS · FORMERS · GRIDS · ETC IN PORCELAIN
DOOR FURNITURE SINCE 1869
ESTABLISHED 1843

Tipton.
STAFFS.

TRADE MARK

OUR REF   YOUR REF   DATE

C.A.L. Harris

BULLERS LIMITED.
MANUFACTURERS.
TELEGRAPH ENGINEERS,
AND CONTRACTORS TO
RAILWAY COMPANIES,
POST OFFICE TELEGRAPHS,
HOME, COLONIAL & FOREIGN GOVERNMENTS.

BIRMINGHAM TELEPHONE 232.
TELEGRAPHIC ADDRESS. "BULLERS BIRMINGHAM".

HANLEY — JOINERS SQUARE WORKS.
DUDLEY — PHŒNIX WORKS.

LONDON. — 32 & 33, QUEEN STREET. E.C.
GLASGOW — 224, INGRAM STREET.

Registered Office, Sherlock Street Works,

Birmingham, 14th Dec. 1894.

From **BULLERS LIMITED,** ~~SHERLOCK STREET WORKS,~~ *Tipton* **BIRMINGHAM,**

MANUFACTURERS OF CHINA DOOR FURNITURE FOR HOME AND FOREIGN MARKETS. MORTARS & PESTLES, &c., &c.

TELEGRAMS—"BULLERS, BIRMINGHAM."   **Telegraph Insulators.**   BIRMINGHAM TELEPHONE, No. 232.

CONTRACTORS TO GOVERNMENT AND POST OFFICE TELEGRAPHS, RAILWAY AND TELEGRAPH COMPANIES.

ESTABLISHED IN DEVONSHIRE 1843.
REMOVED TO STAFFORDSHIRE 1860.

BIRMINGHAM—SHERLOCK STREET WORKS.
HANLEY—JOINERS' SQUARE WORKS.
DUDLEY—PHŒNIX WORKS.

LONDON—32 & 33, QUEEN STREET, E.C.
GLASGOW—224, INGRAM STREET.

To   The Registrar of Joint Stock Companies,   Sept.27th 1895.
          Somerset House,London,W.C.

          Dear Sir,

                    We beg to enclose you a formal Notice that we have closed

          our Birmingham Branch at Sherlock St.,and transferred the

          business,together with our business from Dudley,to our New

          Works at Tipton,where until finally decided by the Directors,

          our Head Office will be situated.

                              We are,Dear Sir,
                                   Yours faithfully,
                         P. PRO BULLERS LIMITED

                         T H Simmonds SECRETARY.

A selection of company letterheads. The top one was designed by Colin Harris.

users claimed that they produced good results in cooking. Little advertising of the products in the trade press appears to have taken place and other tableware companies such as Hornsea, Hostess Tableware and Ulster Ceramics show very similar products in their advertisements of the time. It was clearly a competitive market. The Milton Brook products were more expensive than some of the other makes - perhaps their target market preferred a cheaper product.

Door furniture and beer pump handles were still in production until the second half of the 20th century. Catalogues show that these products were manufactured under the name of Bullers Engineering at the Tipton site. These catalogues also claim that the items were *"hand painted and decorated"* but, in reality, most of the decoration seems to have been lithographed. For a period, the door finger plates were cast at Milton, but some difficulty was experienced in preventing them from warping. Dust pressing was tried as an alternative method, but blanks were also bought in from A.G. Hackney, also of Stoke-on-Trent. Blank finger plates and beer pump handles were sent to the Spode factory in Stoke-upon-Trent where they were transfer printed with traditional blue and white decoration. One such finger plate is still to be seen in situ on a door at the Spode Works in Stoke.

The range included bathroom accessories such as porcelain towel holders, soap dishes and handles. They included use of the trade name "Tiara" and were decorated with lithographed flowers. One girl was employed at Milton applying lithographs. It is not clear how the work was divided between the two sites.

At the 1981 International Spring Fair at the N.E.C. in Birmingham the company had a presence on two separate stands. In the catalogue, Milton Brook Pottery described their wares as *"Freezer to oven to table cookware made of pure porcelain and individually cartoned in attractive boxes specially designed for both export and home trade."* Bullers Staffordshire (operating from Tipton) had a separate stand showing *"A complete range of decorated porcelain door furniture and bathroom fittings in various designs together with an attractive display of cut and plain crystal glass door furniture. Traditional decorated porcelain beer pump handles and porcelain mortars and pestles for the kitchen enthusiast."*[3]

These mortars and pestles were still being made at Milton up until the closure in 2001. The trade name Milton Brook was adopted by Wade who were part of the same group of companies and they have continued to manufacture and market the same mortars and pestles under this name at their Burslem factory.

By 1984 the Milton Brook Pottery name no longer appeared in the trade listings for pottery and tableware, suggesting that the company's commitment to this new range ended about that time.

The production of ash trays was carried out briefly by die pressing. These products were not particularly attractive and, as with their sister company Taylor Tunnicliff, Bullers may have produced these as test pieces, salesmen's samples or gifts rather than as a commercial venture. They were not marked.

CLOSURE

In 2000 the decision was made to cease production at Milton and to buy in from other companies, many of them overseas competitors. The financial situation of the company had been in decline throught the 1970s and the market for porcelain insulators appeared to be contracting each year. Insulators which had been designed to last forever did not need to be replaced and so the company suffered for their own high standards of quality. None of the other new products which the company had tried could fill this gap. As competition from overseas and from insulators made from glass and composite materials continued to erode Bullers' market it was inevitable that the contracting workforce and plant would soon become uneconomic.

On 27th July 2001 the factory finally closed ending 83 years of production at Milton. Some staff were transferred to Wade Ceramics' Royal Works at Burslem where mortars, pestles and insulators continued to be produced.[4] Others were relocated to new office premises at Stone.

The name of Bullers will, however, continue to be remembered. Collectors already seek out both Bullers' insulators and the products of their art pottery studio. As they form part of so many large power, rail and telephone installations, their insulators will continue to be in use and part of peoples' lives throughout the world for many decades into the future.

REFERENCES

1. Tableware reference book 1980. International Trade Publications Ltd.
2. Wade Ceramics. Advertising literature for Milton Brook - mortars and pestles. 2002.
3. International Spring Fair 1981. Catalogue.
4. End of an era as mill shuts down in The Sentinel 27th July 2001. p.13

Part of a 1977 exhibition at Gladstone Working Pottery Museum entitled *Art Among the Insulators*. Section showing range of bar fittings, door furniture and mortars and pestles.

C. 1940

C. 1940

BULLERS LIMITED

KEEP THIS DEPARTMENT TIDY !

This 1960s poster reflects a change in atmosphere following the merger with Taylor Tunnicliff.

Appendix I

Text of illuminated manuscript presented to John Waugh Harris on the occasion of his 21st birthday 1894

Presented to Mr. J.W. Harris

Dear Sir,

On behalf of the whole of the Employes [sic] of Bullers Limited, at Joiners Square Works, we, the undersigned Committee appointed by them, desire to congratulate you upon the attainment of your 21st Birthday.

Many of us who have been in the employ of the firm during the whole time of your esteemed father's connection with the business, remember with gratification the kind consideration always extended to us by him; and we are proud to be able to put on record here, the high reputation which the business has attained, largely by his careful judgment and sound business principles; it is our sincere wish that you may be enabled not only to help to maintain the business in its present efficient state, but to foster its further growth and development.

We are glad of the opportunity of recording our satisfaction at the honourable treatment which has invariably been given to the work-people by the members of the firm; but in the closer relationship of Employer and Employed, in which your father has been for many years the personal representative of the firm, we have great pleasure in testifying to the generous and straightforward manner in which he has acted in all cases that have come up for settlement in connection with our labour, and that there has never been a serious dispute between us in the history of the firm, and we trust that the feeling of sincere attachment and affection with which your father is regarded by us may be continued with yourself.

We therefore ask your acceptance of the accompanying Gold Watch & Set of Hunting Harness with the earnest wish that you may be spared to live a long and useful life, and that with the possibilities before you, and the example set you by your respected father, you may realize your responsibilities and strengthen that feeling of sincere affection which has caused us to offer you this token of our esteem, so justly gained during the period you have been amongst us.

We are, dear Sir, Yours respectfully,

JOSEPH GRICE	THOMAS JONES	JAMES JACKSON	WILLIAM TAYLOR
JOHN WESTON	BORISTON SMITH	JOHN NUNNS	WILLIAM COTTON
ROBERT WARDLE	WILLIAM RATHBONE	CHARLES BEARDMORE	JOHN MOULDS
JOHN BENTLEY	GEORGE BOWERING	GEORGE JOHNSON	CHARLES BICKERTON
JOSEPH LOVATT	GEORGE DAVIS	JOHN BURNDRED	DANIEL WHETTON

Chairman:	Treasurer:	Secretary:
Isaac B. Pennell	J.K. Ashworth	E.W. Boote

August 28th 1894

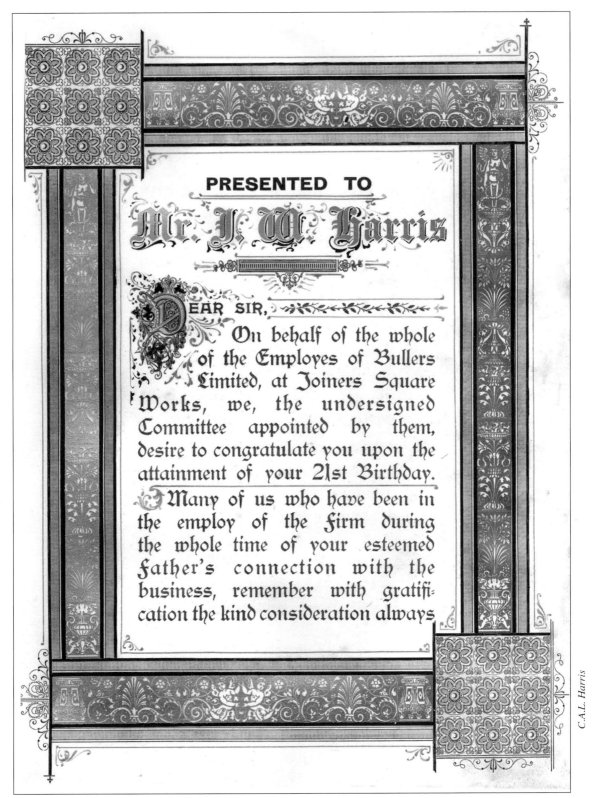

PRESENTED TO
Mr. J. W. Harris

DEAR SIR,

On behalf of the whole of the Employes of Bullers Limited, at Joiners Square Works, we, the undersigned Committee appointed by them, desire to congratulate you upon the attainment of your 21st Birthday.

Many of us who have been in the employ of the Firm during the whole time of your esteemed Father's connection with the business, remember with gratification the kind consideration always

C.A.L. Harris

First page of an illuminated manuscript presented to John W. Harris by the employees of Bullers in 1894. A full transcript of the text is opposite.

China Door Furniture

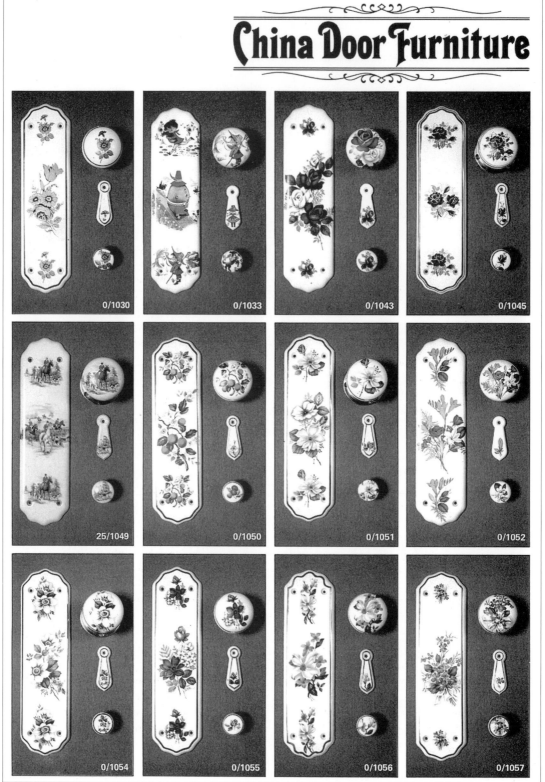

C.A.L. Harris

From Bullers' Engineering catalogue.

Appendix 2
LIST OF BULLERS PATENTS

3.5.1849	12599	Manufacture of earthenware	Thomas Wentworth Buller
28.11.1862	3194	Improvements in spur supporting rings for fixing plates, dishes and other like articles in glost ovens.	Wentworth Buller
29.4.1870	1232	Improvements in attaching door and other knobs and handles to spindles and in the manufacture of door and other knobs and handles, parts of which improvements may be applied to the manufacture of the terminal ornaments of metallic furniture and other articles	Ernest Wentworth Buller
26.1.1871	211	Attaching knobs and handles to spindles	Ernest Wentworth Buller
28.11.1881	5184	Improvements in knobs and in their attachment to spindles	Ernest Wentworth Buller
30.7.1884	10754	Improvements in lock spindles and the method of attaching the same to knobs and handles	Ernest Wentworth Buller
25.6.1891	10817	Improved apparatus or appliance for use in supporting ceramic-ware in enamel-kilns whilst being fired	Isaac Pennell and John Thomas Harris
8.6.1892	10823	Improvements in the construction and attachment of insulators for telegraph, telephone and such like purposes	Ernest Wentworth Buller
11.6.1892	11032	An improvement in insulating supports for electrical conductors led in culverts	John Thomas Harris
3.11.1893	20883	Telegraphic, telephonic	Bullers Ltd.
2.4.1894	6554	Metallic tubular telegraph poles	Bullers Ltd.
2.2.1895	2373	Improvements in the socket joints of metallic telegraph poles	Bullers Ltd. and Edward John Chambers
13.6.1895	11544	Improvements in the manufacture of the insulator arms of telegraph poles and poles for carrying conductors of electricity generally	Bullers Ltd. and Edward John Chambers
11.7.1895	13387	A new or improved tool or appliance for cutting screw threads in hollow articles of clay or other soft materials	Bullers Ltd. and John Thomas Harris
26.1.1903	1830	Improvements in or additions to the third rail insulators of electrical railways	Bullers Ltd. and Edward John Chambers
14.8.1903	17630	Improvements in or addititons to the socket joints of metallic telegraph poles and other like poles	Bullers Ltd. and Edward John Chambers
24.4.1907	9515	Improvements in insulators for telegraph poles and the like	Bullers Ltd and Edward Haward Chambers
16.2.1909	3798	Improvements in means for use in the manufacture of telegraph and like insulators	George William Carr and Bullers Ltd.
26.5.1909	12477	Improvements in electric insulators	Bullers Ltd. and Hubert Dagnall
6.10.1910	23153	Improved method of supporting electric cables or wires and means therefor	Bullers Ltd. and Hubert Dagnall
20.10.1910	24368	Improvements in joints for telegraph poles and the like	Bullers Ltd. and Hubert Dagnall
8.2.1911	3272	Improvements in electric insulators	Bullers Ltd. and George Victor Twiss
2.3.1911	5301	Improvements in or relating to the tensioning of wires, rods or the like	Bullers Ltd. and John Whitehouse Jones
19.8.1911	18680	Improvements in or relating to the attachment of insulator carrying arms to telegraph and like poles	Bullers Ltd and Edward Haward Chambers
16.11.1911	25518	Improvements in footsteps for telegraph posts or poles and other like posts or poles	Bullers Ltd. and John Whitehouse Jones
2.12.1911	26980	Improvements in or relating to the attachment of tubular insulator carrying arms to telegraph and like poles	Bullers Ltd and Edward Haward Chambers

9.2.1912	3335	Improvements in means for holding electrical insulators and conductors Bullers Ltd. and George Victor Twiss
11.3.1912	5992	Telegraph pole brackets Bullers Ltd
13.3.1912	6286/6287	Improvements in electric insulators Bullers Ltd. and George Victor Twiss
18.11.1914	22691	Improvements in footsteps for telegraph and the like poles, brackets for shelving and other like brackets Bullers Ltd. and Bertie Wood
9.12.1914	23761	Improvements in joints for metallic telegraph posts and other like posts or poles Bullers Ltd and Hubert Charles Rayner Dagnall
26.8.1915	12276	Improvements in or relating to the attachment of insulator carrying arms to telegraph and like poles Bullers Ltd. and Hubert Charles Rayner Dagnall
1916	101233	Improved means for supporting and insulating electric lines Bullers Ltd. and George Victor Twiss
17.10.1918	119829	Improvements in pillar insulators George Victor Twiss and Bullers Ltd.
1919	124321	Improved means for connecting materials having different coefficients of expansion George Victor Twiss and Bullers Ltd.
22.11.20	GB154267	Improved turning attachment for use on lathes Gilbert Harvey Harris
6.2.22	GB174766	Improvements in or relating to lathes Gilbert Harvey Harris
31.3.24	GB213655	Improvements in or relating to insulators for supporting high-tension transmission cables and the like Horace Sydney Newman & Richard John Percival Briggs
16.7.25	GB236687	Improvements in apparatus for pugging or extruding plastic potter's clay and the like Edward John Hackley & Frank Reed Pennell
28.7.25	GB237357	Improvements in machines for sieving semi-plastic pottery clay, dust and like material Edward John Hackley
25.6.28	GB292689	Improvements in or relating to insulator couplings and chains of insulators Percy Rock
27.9.29	GB320036	Improvements in or relating to clamps for holding cables or the like John Gordon Miller
12.12.29	GB322682	Improvements in or relating to insulators John Gordon Miller
22.4.30	GB328229	Improvements in or relating to suspension clamps for cables John Gordon Miller
21.5.30	GB329985	Improvements in or relating to cotter-pins for retaining suspension-pins in insulator hoods Horace S Newman
2.9.30	GB249630	Improvements in or relating to wired wireless systems Colin Grant Lewis
22.12.30	GB340554	Improvements in or relating to overhead electricity supply systems and fittings for making multiple connections to the aerial electric lines John Edwin Stewart & Reginald Thomas Norton
9.4.31	GB346752	Improvements in or relating to cable clamps John Gordon Miller
21.4.31	GB347591	Improvements in and relating to fittings for anchoring wires, cables & the like John Edwin Stewart & Reginald Thomas Norton
28.4.31	GB347612	Improvements in or relating to the manufacture of ceramic articles such as insulators John Elvine Harris
22.6.31	GB351062	Improvements in or relating to electric cable clamps John Gordon Miller
12.11.31	GB361372	Improvements in or relating to suspension clamps for electric cables John Gordon Miller
31.3.32	GB369671	Improvements in or relating to devices for indicating when a flash-over has occurred across an insulator or chain of insulators Hubert Charles Rayner Dagnall
19.4.32	GB371357	Improvements in or relating to protective devices for electric insulators Hubert Charles Rayner Dagnall

2.8.32	GB378021	Improvements in or relating to clamps for electric cables John Gordon Miller
15.8.32	GB378882	Improvements in or relating to electric insulators
		Joseph Lustgarten Langton
18.4.33	GB391185	Improvements in or relating to electric cable clamps
		John Gordon Miller
16.5.33	GB392545	Improvements in or relating to attachments for securing electric insulator-supports to chimney stacks, pillars, or the like John Gordon Miller
3.8.33	GB396244	Improvements in or relating to electric insulators
		Hubert Charles Rayner Dagnall
2.5.34	GB409694	Improvements in or relating to electric insulators George Perrins
15.2.35	GB367015	Improvements in or relating to fastenings for securing wires, cables or the like to supports Charles Alfred Murray Henderson
5.4.35	GB426584	Improvements in or relating to pin-type electric insulators
		Gilbert Harvey Harris & Hubert Charles Rayner Dagnall
27.8.36	GB452678	Improvements in or relating to carriers for attaching overhead electric power cables to insulators Hubert Charles Rayner Dagnall
7.9.36	GB453143	Improvements in or relating to electric insulators
		Hubert Charles Rayner Dagnall
29.4.39	GB484020	Improvements in or relating to electric insulators
		Hubert Charles Rayner Dagnall
16.5.39	GB506051	Improvements in or relating to electric insulators
		William George Robinson
16.5.39	GB505981	Improvements in or relating to electric insulators
		William George Robinson
18.7.39	GB509606	Improvements in or relating to electric insulators
		Hubert Charles Rayner Dagnall
12.8.40	GB524663	Improvements in or relating to electric insulators
		Hubert Charles Rayner Dagnall
5.12.40	GB530114	Improvements in or relating to wireless aerials John Ernest Nickless
17.1.41	GB532117	Improvements in or relating to electric insulators Gilbert Harvey Harris
28.7.41	GB538284	Improvements in or relating to cotter pins for retaining suspension pins in insulator hoods Charles Claude Cockbain, Hubert Dagnall & George Perrins
11.2.49	GB617834	Improvements in or relating to electric insulators George Perrins
11.2.49	GB617833	Improvements in or relating to electric insulators George Perrins
22.2.49	GB618484	Improvements in or relating to electric insulators
		William George Robinson & George Perrins
19.4.50	GB635814	Improvements in or relating to gas-filled electric insulators George Perrins
17.5.50	GB637218	Improvements in or relating to electric insulators
		Joseph Lustgarten Langton
27.9.50	GB643814	Improvements in or relating to electric insulators having semi-conducting glazes
		George Perrins
27.11.51	US2576723	Electric insulator having potential drop controlling means George Perrins
5.12.51	GB662322	Improvements in or relating to electric insulators William Henry Hatfield
14.4.54	GB707347	Improvements in or relating to anchoring clamps for cables
		Frank John Neve & Alfred Harold Tolley
21.8.57	GB781523	Improvements in or relating to assemblages of bats and separating pillars for supporting ceramic ware during firing Thomas Rhead
19.4.61	GB865835	Improvements in or relating to jaws for crushing apparatus
		Harold Clarke
7.12.77	GB1494203	Kiln furniture particular crank structures Horace Gilbert Fellows

BULLERS LIMITED, 6 Laurence Pountney Hill, Cannon St., London.

All Insulators supplied in White Porcelain, unless other color asked for.

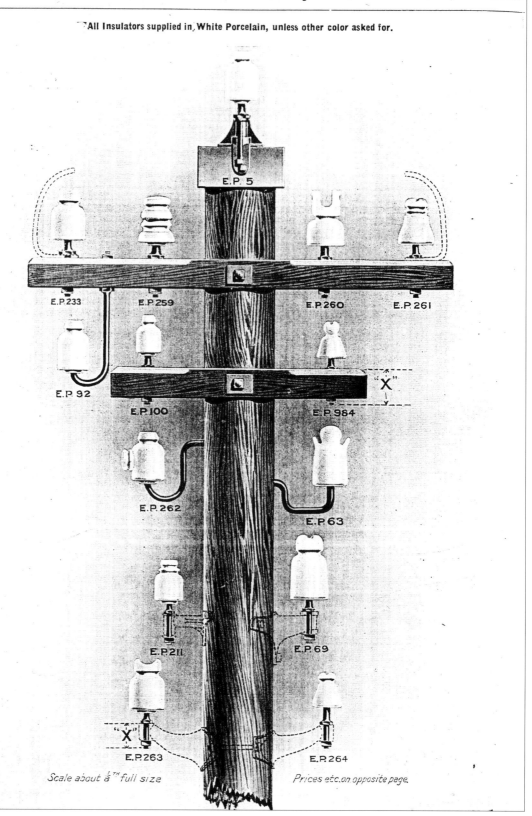

Scale about ⅛ᵀᴴ full size   Prices etc. on opposite page.

Appendix 3
SAMPLE OF BULLERS' CUSTOMERS DURING THE PERIOD 1886-1905

Compiled from early pattern books for insulators, electrical accessories and other company products, this listing highlights the volume of Bullers' business and its international spread.

A.C.M. & Co.
Acme Electric Works 1889
Agent General of South Australia
Anglo American Brush 1888
Anglo-American Brush Electric Light Corp. 1886
A. Balfour & Co.
Barnett, Barnard & Co. 1891
Bartrum Pretyman & Mumford
Baxendale & Co. 1892
J. Beausire & Co. 1893
J. & M.P. Bell & Co., Glasgow
Binswanger 1889
Bishop & Stonier, Hanley, Stoke-on-Trent 1901
Boinader Bros., Granada 1875.
W. Boulton Ltd. 1901, 1903-4
Bowley and Bristow, London
Caledonian Railway Co.
Callender's Bitumen Co. 1894
Castel & Latta, Glasgow. 1875
The Chili Tel. Co. Ltd
Chloride Electrical Co. 1894
R. Cochrane & Co. Britannia, Glasgow
Consolidated Telephone Co. 1895
Consolidated Telephone Construction Maintenance Co 1883
Copthall Stoves Ltd. 1899
Crompton & Co. 1897
Dunn Bennett & Co. Boothen Works, Hanley, 1879
East Tel. Co.
Edison & Swan United Electric Light Co. 1894
Electrical Accessories Co. 1891
Electrical Engineering Corporation 1890
Fernand Espir 1893
Exchange Telegraph Co. 1891
S.Z. de Ferranti 1892 and 1888
Findlay Durham and Brodie 1898
Franco Torrome 1875
W.N. Froy
Fry Miers & Co.
John C Fuller & Son, Bow, London
General Electric Co. 1897
Glasgow and South Western Railway 1899
Golden Hill Cobalt Co.
William Graves & Co., Glasgow 1881
Great Central Railway 1897
Great Eastern Railway Co. 1886
Great North of Scotland Railway 1893
Great Western Railway Co.
Gulcher Electric Light & Power Co. 1894
J Hall & Son 1909
Hammond & Co. 1891
Hardy Peake & Co., Wolverhampton 1878
F.W. Harris   1902, 1911
W.T. Henley & Co. 1870, 1876
H.H. The Nizam's Telephone Dept. 1898
G. Hill 1897
India Rubber Co., Silvertown 1884
India Rubber Gutta Percha Co (Silvertown) 1893
International Okonite Co. 1892
Jobson Bros., Dudley 1877, 1884
Richard Johnson & Nephew, Manchester

Keeling & Walker, Stoke-on-Trent
Kirkham (i.e. Siemens)
Lancashire & Yorkshire Railway Co.
Lever Bros. 1897
Liverpool Electric Co. 1893
London Electric Supply Corporation 1889
Manchester Edison Swan Co. Ltd 1892
Matthewson & Co., London
W. McGeoch 1897
McKenzie & Holland, Worcester 1876
McLean Bros. & Rigg 1881
W. McWhirter 1893
J. & G. Meakin, Stoke-on-Trent
D. Methven & Sons
L.C. Muirhead & Co. Aug 1889
Munroe and Anderson
Munro's Electrical Manufacturing Co. 1897
Mutual Tel. Co. 1892
Natal Tel. Co. 1895
National Telephone Co. Aug 1886, 1892
T.G. Neville & Co. 1888
North Staffordshire Railway
Old Hall Company, Stoke-on-Trent
Oliver & Co. 1897
Joseph Oppenheimer, Manchester 1882
Oriental Tel. Co. Ltd 1893
Patterson & Cooper 1890
Poole & White 1889
Rahr and Raundrup, Manchester 1877
Reid Bros., Birmingham
Reynolds Carter & Reynolds
Emil Richter 1893
G.J. Rogers 1878
Safety Concentric Wiring Co. 1899
Julius Sax & Co. 1892
E. Scott and Mountain 1893
Selby Bigge & Co. 1897
Shuttleworth, Erith, Kent
Siemens Bros. & Co. Ltd. 1884
Slater & Co,. Melbourne
South Devon Railway Co.
Spagnoletti & Crookes 1889
Stafford Coal & Iron Co. 1905
Standard Wire Co. 1897
J. Stiff & Sons 1895
Stone & Co. 1893
Taylor Tunnicliff & Co. 1895
Tel. Co. Ireland 1892
Tel. Co. of Egypt 1893
G.A. Tolzmann & Co. 1894
Ullathorne & Edmondson 1892
United Telephone Co. 1889
Voigt and Haeffner 1892
Walsall Electrical Co. 1897
P. Walters & Co. 1888
W.M. Warden & Co. 1878
Warden Muirhead & Clark, Westminster
Western Electric Co.
Woodhouse & Rawson 1893
Yorkshire Telephone Co.

LISTING BY YEAR OF ORDER

1870 W.T. Henley & Co.
1875 Boinader Bros., Granada
1875 Castel & Latta, Glasgow
1875 Franco Torrome
1876 McKenzie & Holland, Worcester
1877 Jobson Bros., Dudley
1877 Rahr and Raundrup, Manchester
1878 Hardy Peake & Co., Wolverhampton
1878 G.J. Rogers
1878 W.M. Warden & Co.
1879 Dunn Bennett & Co. Boothen Works, Hanley, Stoke-on-Trent
1881 William Graves & Co., Glasgow
1881 McLean Bros. & Rigg
1882 Joseph Oppenheimer, Manchester
1883 Consolidated Telephone Construction Maintenance Co. Ltd.
1884 Siemens Bros. & Co. Ltd.
1886 Anglo-American Brush Electric Light Corp.
1886 Great Eastern Railway Co.
1886 National Telephone Co.
1888 Anglo American Brush
1888 S.Z. de Ferranti
1888 T.G. Neville & Co.
1888 P. Walters & Co.
1889 Acme Electric Works
1889 Binswanger
1889 London Electric Supply Corporation
1889 L.C. Muirhead & Co.
1889 Poole & White
1889 Spagnoletti & Crookes
1889 United Telephone Co.
1890 Electrical Engineering Corporation
1890 Patterson & Cooper
1891 Barnett, Barnard & Co.
1891 Electrical Accessories Co.
1891 Exchange Telegraph Co.
1891 Hammond & Co.
1892 Baxendale & Co.
1892 International Okonite Co.
1892 Manchester Edison Swan Co. Ltd.
1892 Mutual Tel. Co.
1892 Julius Sax & Co.
1892 Tel. Co. Ireland

1892 Ullathorne & Edmondson
1892 Voigt and Haeffner
1893 J. Beausire & Co.
1893 Fernand Espir
1893 Great North of Scotland Railway
1893 India Rubber Gutta Percha Co. Ltd., Silvertown
1893 Liverpool Electric Co.
1893 W. McWhirter
1893 Oriental Tel. Co. Ltd.
1893 Emil Richter
1893 E. Scott and Mountain
1893 Stone & Co.
1893 Tel. Co. of Egypt
1893 Woodhouse & Rawson
1894 Callender's Bitumen Co.
1894 Chloride Electrical Co.
1894 Edison & Swan United Electric Light Co.
1894 Gulcher Electric Light & Power Co.
1894 G.A. Tolzmann & Co.
1895 Consolidated Telephone Co.
1895 Natal Tel Co.
1895 J. Stiff & Sons
1895 Taylor Tunnicliff & Co.
1897 Crompton & Co.
1897 General Electric Co.
1897 Great Central Railway
1897 G. Hill
1897 Lever Bros.
1897 W. McGeoch
1897 Munro's Electrical Manufacturing Co.
1897 Oliver & Co.
1897 Selby Bigge & Co.
1897 Standard Wire Co.
1897 Walsall Electrical Co.
1898 Findlay Durham and Brodie
1898 H.H. The Nizam's Telephone Dept.
1899 Copthall Stoves Ltd.
1899 Glasgow and South Western Railway
1899 Safety Concentric Wiring Co.
1901 Bishop & Stonier, Hanley, Stoke-on-Trent
1901 W. Boulton Ltd.
1902 F.W. Harris
1905 Stafford Coal & Iron Co.
1909 J Hall & Son

WHAT WERE THESE CUSTOMERS BUYING FROM BULLERS?

Year	Customer	Product
1875	Boinader Bros., Granada	S5 insulator
1875	Castel & Latta, Glasgow	S4 insulator
1876	Castel & Latta, Glasgow	P94 insulator
1877	Jobson Bros.	T112 new Post Office insulator
1877	Jobson Bros.	T129 new Post Office insulator
1877	Jobson Bros.	T128 new Post Office terminal
1877	Rahr and Raundrup, Manchester	P131 insulator
1878	Hardy Peake & Co, Wolverhampton	Y143 insulator
1882	John C. Fuller & Son, Bow	T223 'Corrugated insulator'
1882	Jobson Bros.	D184 Canadian insulator
1882	Johnson & Phillips no.41	I213 insulator
1882	Johnson & Phillips no.63	P227 insulator
1883	India Rubber Co.	D38 insulator
1883	Consolidated Telephone Construction Maintenance Co	

Year	Customer	Product
		P3/222 insulator
1884	Jobson Bros.	T241 Canadian Gisborne insulator
1884	Jobson Bros.	D225 insulator
1884	India Rubber Co., Silvertown	D237 insulator
1884	Jobson Bros., Dudley Italian	P238 insulator
1884	Siemens Bros. & Co. Ltd.	Y245 insulator
1886	National Telephone Co.	
		T264 insulator to Mr Coleman's patterns
1888	T.G. Neville & Co.	T10 insulator
1888	P. Walters	P11 insulator
1889	United Telephone Co.	T10 insulator
1889	London Electric Supply Corporation	
		DU176 leading in pipe
1889	Acme Electric Works	EA15 ceiling rose

1889	Spagnoletti & Crookes	EA17 ceiling rose
1889	L.C. Muirhead & Co.	

DU 388 Sadde insulator to go in C.J. culverts for cables

1891	Hammond & Co.	EA447 cap and washer
1892	Tel. Co. Ireland	Y4 insulator
1892	Mutual Tel. Co.	T10 Double Shed Bennett
1892	National Telephone Co. Ltd,	DU479 insulator
1892	Baxendale & Co.	Y481 insulator
1892	Siemens Bros.	T482 insulator
1892	Voigt and Haeffner	

EA73 ceiling rose marked VH15amp

1892	Electrical Accessories Co.	EA671 switch base
1892	Ullathorne & Edmonson	EA481 resistance bars
1892	Julius Sax & Co.	EA864 Copper strip carrier
1893	W McWhirter	Shackle
1893	Keep Bros.	Insulator
1893	India Rubber Gutta Percha Co.	Pulley wheel
1893	Johnson & Phillips	Shackle
1893	Anderson & Munro	Oil insulator
1893	Anderson & Munro	Bobbin
1893	Tel. Co. of Egypt	Shackle
1893	Brush Electrical Engineering Co.	W.P.Reels
1893	Chili Tel. Co. Ltd.	W.P. Insulator
1893	Crompton & Co.	W.P. Insulator
1893	Walsall Electrical Co.	Bobbin
1893	Brush Electrical Co.	Bobbin
1893	Brush Electrical Co.	Reel
1893	Woodhouse & Rawson	P489 insulator for Saltburn lift

1893	Oriental Tel. Co. Ltd.	T509 insulator
1893	India Rubber Gutta Percha Co. Ltd., Silvertown	

Y516 Pulley wheel

1893	General Electric Co.	EA1061 wall plug
1893	Emil Richter	EA1048 cut out
1893	Julius Sax & Co.	EA868 Copper strip separator
1894	Gulcher Electric Light & Power Co.	EA1006 fuse box
1895	Natal Tel. Co.	P619 insulator
1897	Parker	Y738 bobbin
1897	Walsall Electrical Co.	Y740 bobbin
1897	Standard Wire Co.	D742 battery stand
1897	Lever Bros.	P743 insulator
1897	Selby Bigge & Co.	P744 insulator
1897	Lancashire & Yorkshire Railway	Y745 Bobbin
1897	Munro's Electrical Manufacturing Co.	Y746 Reel
1897	General Electric Co.	Y747 Reel
1897	Great Central Railway	

T761 insulator with T129 Cordeaux screw

1898	Findlay Durham and Brodie	P764 insulator
1898	Oriental Telephone Co.	

P771 insulator with T129 Cordeaux screw

1898	H.H.The Nizam's Telephone Dept.	

T794 insulator like T199 with Cordeaux screw

1901	W Boulton Ltd.	Pump ram
1901	Bishop & Stonier	Pump ram
1902	F. W. Harris	Pump ram
1905	Stafford Coal & Iron Co.	Pump ram
1909	J. Hall & Son	Pump ram

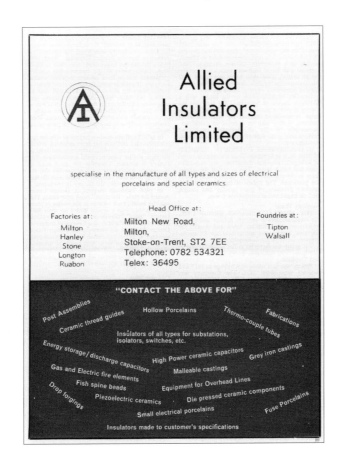

Appendix 4
EXHIBITIONS

From catalogue of Exhibition of BRITISH ART IN INDUSTRY, 1935
GALLERY 1 CERAMICS - TOTAL OF 305 ITEMS

Cat. No.	ITEM	PRICE	DESIGNER
15	Vase, porcelain, grained blue glaze, hand made	15s	
21	Salt cellar, hand made, porcelain, turquoise blue glaze	10s	
26	Horse, hand modelled	5s	Anne Potts
27	Vase, porcelain, grained blue glaze, hand made	£1 1s	
31	Bowl, porcelain, grained blue & bronze glaze, hand made	6s	
32	Vase, porcelain, grained blue glaze, hand made	10s 6d	BSA
37	Man, hard porcelain, hand modelled	5s	Anne Potts
38	Powder bowl & lid, porcelain, tea-leaf glaze, hand made	£1 1s	BSA
39	Horse, hand modelled, porcelain	10s 6d	Anne Potts
43	Vase, porcelain, grained blue glaze, hand made	£1 5s	BSA
46	Vase, porcelain, clouded blue, hand made	15s 6d	
48	Dish, porcelain, clair-de-lune glaze	n.p.	Anne Potts
51	Vase, porcelain, clouded blue glaze, hand made	17s 6d	
54	Vase, porcelain, clair-de-lune glaze, hand made	6s	
55	Jug, porcelain, lavender glaze, hand made	10s 6d	
56	Vase, porcelain, clair-de-lune glaze, hand made	£1 1s	
94	Rabbit, hard porcelain, hand modelled	5s	Anne Potts
96	Monkey, hard porcelain, hand modelled	10s 6d	Anne Potts
99	Vase, porcelain, tea-leaf glaze, hand made	15s	
104	Vase, porcelain, cornelian damask glaze, hand made	15s 6d	
107	Plaque, porcelain yellow celadon, hand made	10s 6d	
108	Vase, porcelain, cornelian damask glaze, hand made	15s 6d	
109	Vase, porcelain, celadon glaze, hand made	15s	
112	Vase, porcelain, cornelian damask glaze, hand made	10s 6d	
120	Plaque, "Aurora", porcelain, hand made	12s 6d	
122	Plaque, porcelain, celadon glaze, hand made	10s 6d	Anne Potts
170	Vase, porcelain, yellow grey glaze,crystalline effects, hand made	5s	
180	Vase, porcelain, rose-leaf green glaze, hand made	£1 5s	
181	Vase, porcelain, mottled crystalline green, hand made	15s	
182	Vase, porcelain, mottled green, hand made	15s	
183	Vase, porcelain, celadon glaze, hand made	10s 6d	Anne Potts
184	Vase, porcelain, mottled crystalline green glaze, hand made	£1 1s	
186	Dish, porcelain, mottled crystalline green glaze, hand made	6s	Anne Potts

Cat. No.	ITEM	PRICE	DESIGNER
187	Vase, porcelain, mottled green crystalline glaze, hand made	3s 6d	
188	Vase, porcelain, pale green glaze, hand made	5s	
206	Vase, porcelain, rose-leaf green glaze, hand made	17s 6d	
209	Plaque, porcelain, sea-green glaze, hand made	12s 6d	
211	Vase, porcelain, rose-leaf green glaze, hand made	15s 6d	
213	Vase, porcelain, sea-green glaze, hand made	7s 6d	
215	Vase, porcelain, sea-green glaze, hand made	7s 6d	
218	Man, hard porcelain, hand modelled	5s	Anne Potts
219	Powder bowl & lid, porcelain, mottled green glaze, hand made	£1 1s	BSA
220	Elephant, hard porcelain, hand modelled	10s 6d	Anne Potts
227	Minstrel, porcelain, hand modelled	10s 6d	Anne Potts
229	Waiter, porcelain, hand modelled	10s 6d	Anne Potts
242	Vase, hard porcelain, hare's fur glaze, hand made	15s 6d	
244	Vase, hard porcelain, honey glaze, hand made	15s	
246	Vase, hard porcelain, old ivory glaze, hand made	15s	
249	Elephant	15s	
257	Vase, hard porcelain, hare's fur glaze, hand made	15s	
263	Powder bowl & lid, porcelain, hare's fur glaze, hand made	£1 1s	BSA
265	Vase, hard porcelain, flamed blue, hand made	10s 6d	Anne Potts
270	Vase, porcelain, flambe, hand made	£2 2s	
272	Bowl, hard porcelain, bronze glaze, hand made	£1 1s	
274	Vase, hard porcelain, bronze glaze, hand made	15s 6d	
275	Vase, hard porcelain, bronze glaze, hand made	£1 1s	BSA
282	Hare, porcelain, hand modelled	7s 6d	Anne Potts
284	Plaque, hard porcelain, pale green & brown leather glaze, hand made	10s 6d	

From catalogue of items for Council of Industrial Design "BRITAIN CAN MAKE IT" Exhibition, 1946. Manufactured by Bullers Ltd for Heal's (Wholesale & Export) Ltd, 196 Tottenham Court Rd, London WI

Availability code: for Home Trade now =1, soon = 2, later = 3; for Export now = A, soon = B, later = C

CAT.NO.	DESCRIPTION	SHAPE	ARTIST	AVAILABILITY
503	Vase	270	Agnete Hoy	1 A
504	Dish	251	Agnete Hoy	1 A
505	Candlesticks	391	Agnete Hoy	1 A
506	Small vase	163	Agnete Hoy	1 A
507	Dish	257	Agnete Hoy	1 A
508	Dish	256	Agnete Hoy	1 A

509	Bowl	283	Agnete Hoy	1 A
510	Small dish	154	Agnete Hoy	1 A
511	Small dish	309	Agnete Hoy	1 A
512	Vase	207	Agnete Hoy	1 A
513	Tall celadon vase	396	Agnete Hoy	1 A
514	Black glazed vase	270	Agnete Hoy	1 A
515	Small dish	256	Agnete Hoy	1 A
516	Ashtray	305	Agnete Hoy	1 A
517	Chamois	216	Agnete Hoy	1 A
518	Giraffe	193	Agnete Hoy	1 A
519	Celadon deer	196	Agnete Hoy	1 A
520	Celadon calf	199	Agnete Hoy	1 A

Exhibits 521-526 are banded iron decorated ware

521	Mixing bowl size one	P225	Agnete Hoy	3 C
522	Stewpot size two	P179	Agnete Hoy	3 C
523	Jug	P229	Agnete Hoy	3 C
524	Bowl size four	P316	Agnete Hoy	3 C
525	Casserole size O	P234	Agnete Hoy	3 C
526	Stewpot size O	P330	Agnete Hoy	3 C

Exhibits 527-530 are glazed dark brown

527	Eared dish	P225	Agnete Hoy	3 C
528	Jug	P230	Agnete Hoy	3 C
529	Small jug	P322	Agnete Hoy	3 C
530	Covered jug	P223	Agnete Hoy	3 C

Potters exhibited in *'THE COUNTRY'* Pavilion at the Festival of Britain 1951

Anita [sic] Hoy, Bullers Ltd Milton Stoke-on-Trent

James Rushton, Bullers Ltd Milton Stoke-on-Trent

The Potteries Museum & Art Gallery

BIBLIOGRAPHY

HISTORY OF THE BULLER AND HARRIS FAMILIES

Harris, Nigel. *The Yarlet Story.* 1993
Powell, Geoffrey. *Buller: a scapegoat? A life of General Sir Redvers Buller* 1839-1908. Leo Cooper, 1994
Vivian, John Lambrick. *Visitations of the County of Cornwall*
Wagner, Anthony. *English Genealogy.* 2nd ed. Phillimore, 1972

Journals and newspaper articles
Infringement of a patent. Ford v. Buller in *Staffordshire Advertiser* 27th June 1851 p.3
Obituary of John Waugh Harris in *Pottery Gazette and Glass Trades Review* 1st March 1920 p.377
Obituary of Ralph Guy Harris in *Journal of the British Ceramic Society* October 1963 p.104

Other sources
Buller family papers   Devon Record Office, Exeter

ELECTRICAL ENGINEERING, TELEGRAPHY AND INSULATORS

Albers, M. and Tod, J. *Worldwide Porcelain Insulators.* Albers, c.1982
Bakewell F. C. *Electric Science.* Ingram Cooke & Co., 1853
Brent, W.H. *Porcelain Insulators.* The Post Office Green Papers no.10. 1934
Neal, W. Keith. *Searching for Railway Telegraph Insulators.* Signal Box Press, c.1982
Pope, Frank L. *Modern practice of the electric telegraph: a handbook.* New York, Russell Brothers,1869
Pope, Dr. M. I. *Aerial Line Insulators.* Unpublished paper, 1985
Shaffner's *Telegraph Companion devoted to the science & art of the Morse American Telegraph* vols. 1 and 2.
                                        Pudney & Russell, 1854
Wade, Major G.A. Manufacture of electrical porcelain in *Cox's Pottery Annual and Glass Trade Year Book.* 1926. p.85

Journal and newspaper articles
The manufacture of insulators in *Electrical Power* March 1905 p. 49-53
Watkin, Ernest. Address to the Ceramic Society in *Pottery Gazette and Glass Trade Review* 1st May 1924. p.835
British electro-technical pottery in *Financial Times* 16th July 1930
The manufacture of porcelain insulators in *The Engineer* 12th June 1931 p.658-9
High voltage porcelain insulators in *Ceramics* June 1967. p.45
Johnson, P. and Robinson, W.G. Development of pottery bodies 'electrical porcelain'. Paper delivered at a meeting of
                        the Pottery Section, Trentham Gardens, Stoke-on-Trent, 22nd October 1974
Bulletin for the History of Insulators and Electrical Ceramics No.2. Gladstone Pottery Museum, Stoke-on-Trent, 1984

Other sources
Bullers' pattern books   City Archives, Stoke-on-Trent
Patents Information Network Birmingham Central Library

BULLERS

Journal and newspaper articles
Fernie, K. & Price, E.E. Bullers change to butane in *Ceramics* November 1969 p.14-22
Two North Staffs insulator factories to be merged in *The Sentinel* 5th May 1972
Take-over bid rejected by shareholders in *The Sentinel* 29th December 1972
New technology brings in orders in *The Sentinel* 17th February 1978
North Staffs company to change name in *The Sentinel* 2nd February 1979
Axe to fall on 150 jobs in *The Sentinel* 21st April 1983
Another A.I. plant to close down in *The Sentinel* 28th June 1983
Bright outlook for city firm in *The Sentinel* 9th April 1985
A.I. firm sold for £2.5m in *The Sentinel* 21st February 1986
Jobs boost for Milton firm in *The Sentinel* 16th June 1987
End of an era as mill shuts down in *The Sentinel* 27th July 2001. p.13

Other media
Ceramic Century. Videotaped recordings of pottery industry workers. Gladstone Pottery Museum, Stoke-on-Trent, 2001

BULLERS' ART POTTERY STUDIO

Batkin, Maureen and Atterbury, Paul. *Art among the Insulators: the Bullers Studio 1932-52.* Catalogue of an exhibition at
                        the Gladstone Pottery Museum, Stoke-on-Trent. 1977.

Journal and newspaper articles
An adventure in porcelain in *Pottery and Glass* August 1947 p.29-31
Atterbury, Paul. Made in England by Bullers in *Antique Collector* February 1977. p.32-36
Cooper, Emmanuel. Agnete Hoy [obituary] in *Independent* 14th April 2000. p.6
Death of potter who created unique work in *Sentinel* 13th April 2000. p.21
Haggar, Reginald. Bullers in *Northern Ceramic Society Echoes and Relections*, 1980. p.21
Hoy, Anita. Art among the insulators in *Ceramic Review* no.69 1981 p.10-11
The Work of Agnete Hoy in *Pottery Gazette and Glass Trades Review* July 1952. p.1096

Other media
National Electronic and Video Archive of the Crafts, University of the West of England. Anita Hoy. Series of interviews 1998

HISTORY OF THE POTTERY INDUSTRY & OTHER COMPANIES

Adams, Brian & Thomas, Anthony. *A Potwork in Devonshire: the history and products of the Bovey Tracey Potteries* 1750-1836. Sayce Publishing, 1996

Casey, Andrew. *20th Century Ceramic Designers in Britain.* Antique Collectors Club, 2001.

Cross, A.J. *Pilkington's Royal Lancastrian Pottery and Tiles.* Richard Dennis, 1980

Furnival, William J. *Explanation of the Staffordshire Potteries slop flint & stone trade calculator.* Allbut & Daniel, 1884

Greene, John. *Brightening the long days: hospital tile pictures.* Tiles & Architectural Ceramics Society, 1987

Haslam, Malcolm. *William Staite Murray.* Crafts Council/Cleveland County Museum Service, 1984.

Huntbach, Alfred. *Hanley: Stoke-on-Trent.* 1910

Jewitt, Llewellyn. *The Ceramic Art of Great Britain.* New edition. Orchard Editions, 1985

Ruscoe, William. *A potter's lot.* Unpublished autobiography. c.1982

Scarratt, William. *Old Times in the Potteries.* Scarratt, 1906

Journals and newspaper articles

Forsyth, G.M. Art education in the Potteries: a manufacturers' forward movement in *Pottery and Glass Record* Feb1921. p.120

Art: its effect upon the pottery industry in *Pottery Gazette and Glass Trade Review* 1st August 1921. p.1219

Art instruction in the Potteries in *Pottery Gazette and Glass Trade Review* 2nd May 1927. p.815

Progress in ceramic art in *Pottery Gazette and Glass Trade Review* 2nd June 1930. p.974

Forsyth, G.M. British art in British industry in *Journal of the Royal Society of Arts* 14 December 1934. p.104

Exhibition at museum in *The Sentinel* 21st June 1938

A venture in Cornish slipware in *Pottery Gazette and Glass Trade Review* May 1950. p.711

Taylor Tunnicliff in *A British Bulletin of Commerce Survey.* November 1954

Rowland, Anna. Business management at the Weimar Bauhaus in *Journal of Design History* v.1 (3-4) 1988. p.153

Eatwell, Ann. Gordon Mitchell Forsyth (1879-1952) - artist, educator and father of art education in the Potteries in *Journal of the Decorative Arts Society* no.13 1989. p.27

Niblett, Kathy. Ten plain years: the British pottery industry 1942-1952 in *Northern Ceramic Society Journal* v.12 1995. p.175-213

Livingstone, Karen A. Science, art & industry: the work of William Burton, Gordon Mitchell Forsyth and Pilkington's Tile and Pottery Company in context in *Ars Ceramica* no.13 1996. p.67

EXHIBITION CATALOGUES

Exhibition of British Industrial Art in Relation to the Home. Catalogue. June 20th-July 12th 1933

Royal Academy. *Exhibition of British Art in Industry.* Catalogue. January-March 1935

Council of Industrial Design. *Britain Can Make It* Exhibition catalogue. H.M.S.O., 1946

Batkin, Maureen and Atterbury, Paul. *Art among the insulators: the Bullers Studio 1932-52.* Catalogue of an exhibition at the Gladstone Pottery Museum, Stoke-on-Trent. 1977

Catalogue. *Reginald Haggar: retrospective exhibition of watercolours 1930-1980.* City Museum & Art Gallery, 1980

International Spring Fair 1981. Catalogue

ARCHIVE SOURCES AND COLLECTIONS

Buller family papers

Heal's archive

Company documents

Bullers' pattern books

Patents Information Network

1881 British Population Census

1901 British Population Census

Devon Record Office, Exeter

National Art Library, Victoria and Albert Museum

Public Record Office, Kew, London

City Archives, Stoke-on-Trent

Birmingham Central Library

TRADE DIRECTORIES

Jones's Mercantile Directory of the Pottery District of Staffordshire 1864 London, 1864.

J.G. Harrod & Co. Postal and Commercial Directory of Staffordshire 1870

Kelly's Directory Birmingham 1876

Kelly's Directory Staffordshire 1884

Keates's Gazetteer and Directory of the Staffordshire potteries: Newcastle and District 1889-90. Keates & Co.

Staffordshire Sentinel Ltd. The Sentinel yearbook 1928

Tableware reference book 1980. International Trade Publications Ltd

COMPANY DOCUMENTS

Wade Ceramics. Advertising literature for Milton Brook - mortars and pestles. 2002

Allied Insulators. Company brochure. c.1980

Taylor Tunnicliff Ltd. Bullers Rings. Promotional leaflet. c.2001

Heal's. Craftsman's Market leaflet. Heal's 1948

Heal's. Cargo of presents for particular people. Heal's 1946 (and other catalogues)

Heal's. Publicity leaflet. 1947

Heal's. Come to the Christmas Fair leaflet. 1947

INDEX

Courtesy of Taylor Tunnicliff Ltd

The turning shop at Milton c. 1925-30

Miniature animal models by Anne Potts.

Noah's Ark by Anne Potts

Courtesy of A & J Marshall

Porcelain vase, Anne Potts c.1936, decorated with black slip carved away in a
Chinese style to reveal the clay underneath.

'Gossips', Earthenware rolled figure group by Anne Potts
whilst a student at Burslem School of Art 1933.
It was exhibited at the 1933 exhibition British Industrial
Art in Relation to the Home.

Courtesy of The Potteries Museum & Art Gallery

Porcelain figure signed EB
(Emmanuel Bah) 1946.
Oatmeal glaze.

Porcelain rolled figure of a girl
(perhaps Joyce Cooper) sticking
handles on cups. Anne Potts c. 1935.

Courtesy of The Potteries Museum & Art Gallery

Porcelain teapot and milk jug by Gordon Forsyth dated 1940.
Crackle glaze and iron oxide stained glazed lid and details.

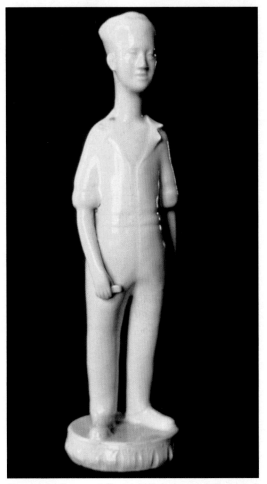

Mrs D. Jeffrey

Porcelain figure of a mother and child designed by
Moira Forsyth and modelled by William Ruscoe
c. 1942. Crackle glaze.

Porcelain figure of Derek Wilshaw modelled by James Rushton.

Porcelain coffee pot with enamel painted decoration,
by James Rushton, c. 1950.

Porcelain rolled figure group by Anne Potts, probably
representing Potts and her art teacher,
Gordon Forsyth c.1935.

Porcelain vase with
copper carbonate
markings, by Agnete
Hoy 1943.

Agnete Hoy Collection Archive

Porcelain bowl with brushed iron oxide decoration
and crackle glaze, by Hilda Hine, c. 1944-52.

Vase, Guy Harris c.1934. The shape is believed to have been cast from a vase in Hanley Museum

Agnete Hoy Collection Archive

Porcelain bowl with bird by Agnete Hoy 1948.
Incised, colour-washed, painted decoration, with clear glaze.

Agnete Hoy Collection Archive

Porcelain bowl by Agnete Hoy 1945. Scratched out pattern with
colour wash and oatmeal glaze.

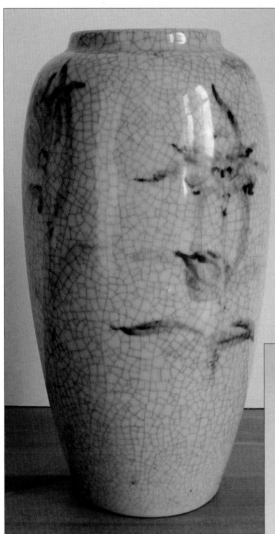

Porcelain vase by Agnete Hoy 1945. Iron and cobalt brushwork and crackle glaze.

Agnete Hoy Collection Archive

Courtesy of The Potteries Museum & Art Gallery

Porcelain vase with flambé glaze, by Guy Harris c.1936.

Agnete Hoy Collection Archive

Porcelain bowl by Agnete Hoy 1942. Iron brushwork and crackle glaze.

Agnete Hoy Collection Archive

Porcelain bowl, Agnete Hoy, 1947. Iron-rich glaze with blue inlay.

Agnete Hoy Collection Archive

Porcelain bowl with hydrangea motif, Agnete Hoy 1949. Iron and cobalt brushwork and oatmeal glaze.

Agnete Hoy Collection Archive

Porcelain bowl with floral motif, Agnete Hoy. Cobalt brushwork and clear glaze.

Agnete Hoy Collection Archive

Porcelain bowl with peony, butterfly and ladybird, by Agnete Hoy. Cobalt brushwork and clear glaze.

Agnete Hoy Collection Archive

Porcelain stem bowl by Agnete Hoy 1946. Chun glaze.

Agnete Hoy Collection Archive

Agnete Hoy Collection Archive

Porcelain figure of young giraffe by Agnete Hoy 1941. Iron brown markings and oatmeal glaze.

Porcelain figure of young camel by Agnete Hoy 1941. Pink copper markings and blue celadon glaze.

Porcelain bowl by Robert Jefferson 1951, with painted decoration.

Porcelain bowl by James Rushton 1945. Cobalt painted decoration and clear glaze.

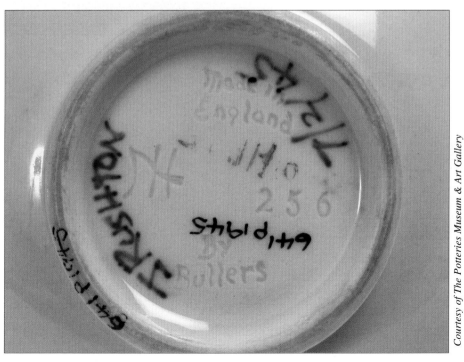

Underside of porcelain bowl by James Rushton showing the standard Bullers'
studio mark and his own date and signature.

Porcelain vase by Agnete Hoy 1945.
Northern green celadon glaze.

Bullers' door fingerplate, underglaze
printed by Spode Ltd, c. 1960.

Porcelain dish decorated
by Hilda Hine c. 1944-52.
Iron brushwork and
painted mark - H.

Agnete Hoy Collection Archive

Courtesy of The Potteries Museum & Art Gallery

Top shelf: Bullers' porcelain jugs and mugs c. 1935.
Bottom shelf: Porcelain vases 1940s.

Porcelain vase with brushed iron oxide decoration, Leslie West c. 1950.

Right: Porcelain mug with enamel painted decoration, by Agnete Hoy, 1947.

Below: Porcelain stewpot with iron oxide bands, designed by Agnete Hoy, c. 1950.

Milton Brook pestles and mortars as manufactured for Wade at Milton in 2002.